MAX MILLER
The Cheeky Chappie

MAX MILLER
The Cheeky Chappie

John M East

W. H. ALLEN · LONDON
A Howard & Wyndham Company
1977

Printed and bound by
The Garden City Press Limited,
Letchworth, Hertfordshire SG6 1JS,
for the publishers, W H Allen & Co. Ltd,
44 Hill Street, London W1X 8LB

ISBN 0491 02260 3

Contents

With grateful acknowledgement to T V Blackstone, whose help in the research of this book and editorial guidance were very valuable.

I owe thanks and appreciation to Mrs Kathleen Miller, the widow of Max Miller, and to his brother, Percy, his sister, Elsie, many correspondents and those people I interviewed.

My thanks are also due to Mrs Miller for allowing me to quote Max Miller's act in chapter 2 : The Performer, and for the lyrics on pages 90, 91 and 149.

John M East, 1977

List of Illustrations

I Setting the Scene

THERE HAS NEVER been a better description of a music-hall artist than 'The Cheeky Chappie'. Over six feet tall, with wide shoulders and narrow hips, Max Miller's fresh pink complexion rivalled that of a baby. His beautiful yet wicked blue eyes suggested roguery and the delights of sex. He looked fresh, as if he had the tang of Brighton air about him. He wore gloriously coloured plus fours, with a jacket to match; a white shirt; an enormous tie and a white trilby placed jauntily to one side of his head. He sported a giant diamond ring and sometimes a cane, encrusted with diamonds.

Max would stand on the edge of the stage and look outwards as if to say, 'Aren't I amazing?' He used his unashamedly bawdy, rasping voice to tell rapid-fire risqué stories with an ebullience and an almost childish air of naughtiness. He was a grown man with the brazen but engaging impudence of a London street arab. There was much of the confidence of those urchins in Max, of the daring-to-cheek-you, not so much because of any quality of his own that would protect him from reprisal, as because he seemed certain people were too good-natured to be anything but amused. His knack of taking for granted the friendliness of the other party is the first quality of charm.

Max was an ageless Puck, dispensing a strange combination of smut and sentimentality which reflected a vital strain of the British way of life. The older he got the cheekier he became.

In the 1950s variety theatres played tatty revues to sparse

audiences and many young recording artists who topped bills were deficient in stage technique. The drag shows and nude extravaganzas were usually seedy.

It was different when Max Miller was engaged. There were ripples of laughter; gusts of merriment; storms of applause. The Cheeky Chappie produced something to beat the lot. He provoked a positive hurricane of mirth which swept from end to end of a packed auditorium.

His strength lay in the projection of his irrepressible personality. He had a machine-gun mind that could produce the right jokes in the most telling sequence, never allowing anybody to lift their eyebrows and think, 'What's next?' You got the answer long before you could wonder whether you really ought to have laughed at the previous gag. All you knew was, you laughed and liked it.

Max Miller, born Thomas Henry Sargent, dragged himself up from the seediest poverty of Edwardian Brighton. With no proper schooling he learned to live by his wits. No one was sharper in making a crust of bread. From his days of childhood truancy he always had a ready reply. He was incorrigible. Many people sink under such hardship, but Harry Sargent had the determination to break the chains. His fabled meanness in later life may have had roots in his beginning. The poor are usually the most generous but Max, with his acquisitive instinct, counted every penny.

The Brighton of Max Miller's childhood was a town of great contrast. Nowhere was there such a marked difference between rich and poor. Charles Cochran, the Brighton-born impresario, reported Henry Labouchère to have described Brighton as 'four miles long and one mile in depth with a Sassoon at each end, and another in the middle'. The King's friendship with the wealthy family of bankers, and his subsequent patronage of Brighton, made the town a centre of fashion and society.

Behind Brighton's glittering front lay slums as bad as those in any northern industrial town. Max Miller, raised in these slums, would have noticed the extremes of wealth and poverty. He caddied for the gentry on the local golf course; he saw the extravagant rich idling along Marine Parade. Though his arse hung out of his trousers, and he wore his mother's shoes at school, Max aped the nobs by wearing spats. As a ten-year-old ragamuffin he was known to his chums as 'Swanky Sargent'.

Edwardian Brighton, with its rich, who flocked to the Theatre Royal to see the latest successes from the West End stage, also had an entertainment tailor-made for the poor, the music hall, where they could chorus the popular songs of the day. Furthermore there would be several concert parties on the front. Near the Palace Pier, nigger minstrels with blackened faces and straw boaters, striped blazers and white flannels played banjos.

Max often watched these performances and, when he could muster a few pennies, he would climb the gallery steps of the Hippodrome to see the peerless exponent of black-faced minstrelsy, G H Elliott, 'The Chocolate Coloured Coon'. He admitted later in life that Elliott's artistry was his first influence and stimulated his desire for a stage career.

Max's passage as a spectator to that of a performer started on the Brighton front in a concert party. He made his way through engagements in obscure theatres to topping the bill at the London Palladium, as Britain's highest paid star of the variety theatre.

How did Max Miller fit into the context of his time? During his childhood the music hall was at its zenith. It was almost exclusively working class, including its composers, singers and audiences. It gave means of escape to poor people, and in its songs and humour covered the whole spectrum of life. It produced immense personalities in profusion—Dan Leno, Harry Lauder, Little Tich, Marie Lloyd, George Robey, G H Chirgwin, Gus Elen and Vesta Tilley to name but a few.

Originally music hall had a chairman to keep order and make announcements. There was a free and easy atmosphere where the patrons moved about, ate and drank, and if a turn warranted their attention they stopped, looked and listened. This form of entertainment became variety in the 1890s when businessmen cashed in on its appeal and hundreds of theatres were built throughout Britain. Instead of a chairman, a number on the proscenium arch indicated the next artist. Working on a twice-nightly basis, everything was strictly timed, so that the second performance could start without delay.

The attraction of a variety theatre was a succession of different acts on a single programme. Each turn was allotted a running time, possibly only eight minutes. Artists rehearsed and produced themselves. It was necessary to make immediate impact with an audience. An artist with the *vital spark* did a seemingly impossible thing. He appeared to play to one person, whereas in fact he projected his act to hold the attention of everybody present.

When Max Miller went on the stage in 1919 variety was in a state of transition. The great stars of the halls were either dead or in decline. The current top-of-the-bill turns were losing the battle of patronage to the cinema, already the most popular form of entertainment.

Variety theatres, instead of providing the variety implicit in their title, presented revues which were all much the same. They were, in effect, a few acts strung together by a story-line or sketches. They were cheaper to mount than a bill of variety, and for a time the public was deceived. The old stars had been seen too frequently; their material was stale.

Soon, however, revues received mixed receptions. Even if a good production followed an indifferent one, the public had been frightened off, and receipts were negligible. It sometimes took weeks for a theatre to regain lost patronage. Moreover, with revue, the variety theatre lost its greatest attraction, the individuality of the single turn.

Max Miller, in the true tradition of variety, was an individualist. He did not need a story-line, a feed or straight man. He used audience reaction to dictate the speed and content of his act.

In his formative years Max had no alternative but to be trapped within the confines of scripted revues. But Max was no actor and he found difficulty in interpreting a part other than himself.

By sheer chance a few sterling talents arrived on the scene and they could only show off their uniqueness by giving rebirth to a bill of contrasting acts. So it was that the artistry of Max Miller, Jimmy James, Will Hay, Sid Field, George Formby, Flanagan and Allen and Gracie Fields could find expression. These artists postponed the death of variety by thirty years. As a box-office draw, Max Miller lasted longer than any of them, and he was right in saying, 'When I'm dead and gone, the game's finished.'

2 The Performer

Max Miller was described as 'the greatest front-cloth comedian of his time'. That meant he was out there, alone, before the front cloth and he held the attention of an audience for half an hour.

He realised that it is social taboo and personal modesty that makes vulgarity so naughtily attractive. He used his understanding to the limit and better than any other comedian. His world was that of predatory landladies, of doubtful parents, of careful girls who, for ten bob, could be willing girls.

Max played an important part in dispelling the Victorian attitudes of guilt by his sheer naturalness and sense of fun which made that guilt seem absurd. Of course, in the social revolution of the twentieth century, there were many prudes who could not stand Miller, and when he went too near the knuckle he was banned by the BBC.

Max had many imitators, but no equal. His manner was superb. That eagerness to confide in every person in front of him in the way of the best storyteller one might meet in everyday life. The secret of his success was, without doubt, the element of danger. A master of innuendo, everybody wondered just how wicked he was going to be. In fact Max triumphed over the slenderest material by a disarming display of diffident candour and a masterly sense of timing.

No other comedian established contact so quickly. Max used pauses and winks which often meant a great deal more than the words he spoke. He judged every nuance so that the imagination of the audience was ahead of him. A volley of titters finally dissolved into a communal roar as he completed the gag.

He was an intuitive performer. His alert mind and expert judgment allowed him to dig into his vast repertoire of jokes, so that one followed another to suit the mood of the audience. Those shining blue eyes; that stammer through excess of enthusiasm—all formed part of a vital battery that radiated its force through the theatre.

If Max's gags rarely rose above the mildly salacious; if his songs, which he sang in a light and pleasantly modulated voice, were not distinguished; if the little ritual dance was purely frivolous, though executed with grace—all this did not matter. The conglomerate effect made Max Miller a genius.

For thirty years Miller was able to fill a theatre with his name. The secret of most comedians before and after his reign as Britain's top jester is that they are at odds with the world; it is too much for them; troubles overwhelm them. Not Max.

He rearranged the world to suit himself. There was no pathos in Max's comedy. There was nothing unconscious about it. Nor was it at somebody else's expense. We laughed with Max because he meant to be funny and he knew he was succeeding; he was quite sure we admired his cheek; he admired it himself.

Max only had one rival, and that was for a short time. Sid Field was one of the greatest drolls to walk the boards. Sid was the underdog. A mild, surprised man, always doing his best, always failing to understand. 'What a performance!' he would say as he gazed at the chaos of which he was the unwitting cause. Sid Field accepted the blows of the world and the kicks of fortune and came sliding and smiling through. In place of Max Miller's unremitting leer, Sid Field had an intermittent smile. His most remarkable virtue was that his comicality was utterly innocuous.

In the famous Golfing Sketch, when the ball failed to roll in the right direction, he pleaded with it: 'Dear ball ... —' Audiences trembled when his lordly drunk whispered into the ear of a Wren. Was he at last going to fall from his innocent grace, so unusual in a comedian? But no, we breathed again in

14

relief. He had merely been inquiring whether or not Lady Hamilton was a Wren and he got his face slapped for it.

Max Miller, on the other hand, painted the stage as blue as his eyes. His every joke, wheeze, innuendo and reference were variants on the same eternal subject. Arnold Bennett, in the frame of mind in which he reviewed Marie Lloyd at the Tivoli Music Hall on the last night of the year 1909, would certainly not have approved of Max Miller.

'I couldn't see the legendary cleverness of the vulgarity of Marie Lloyd. She was very young and spry for a grandmother. All her songs were variations of the same theme of sexual naughtiness. No censor would ever pass them, and especially he wouldn't pass her winks and her silences.'

But to deny grace and cleanness to an artist's material is not to deny accomplishment to his or her manner. Arnold Bennett himself would have been the first to recognise and salute the extraordinary perfection of Max Miller's technique and timing, and the amazingly quick, lusty, and direct impact of his personality. 'Worse?' he shouted with his incorrigible grin through the loud laughter his latest monstrous sally had evoked. And worse and worse he certainly gave his audience.

Max was large and solid. He brushed aside all the buffeting of destiny as a man flicks a fly off his sleeve. He bestrode trouble with a grin and triumphed over calamity. Brazen, blatant, dressed to dazzle and all out for mischief, he came off victor in any exchange of impudence or repartee.

What endeared Max Miller to his audiences was not only his mischief; it was the amiable way he conducted his offensive. There never was, the house felt, such a cad as the flashy cockney oaf whom he impersonated. But never, likewise, was caddishness such good company, or social aggression so charmingly odious. That roving eye of his, and his easy, knowing smile, were the weapons of a flawless theatrical attack. He was as richly vulgar as a check suit, jewelled fingers and blue pencil japes could make him. Very commonplace, you may say, but full of uncanny cunning. If the righteous had called Max Miller to the stool of repentance, he would have immediately made it his throne.

It surprised many people who had heard Max's material was saucy, to find that, off stage, he was not a vulgar, red-nosed extrovert. In person he was distinguished, and he had decided attractions.

In 1958, during his last performance at the Empress, Brixton, which he visited annually, I went to see him in his dressing room. There was an even stronger suggestion of the dichotomy between Max's public image as a variety performer and the man in private life. To managements and the press he maintained his cocky air, but behind the façade lay an entirely different personality. I saw him stripped of his brash and brazen image. In his round, genial face lurked cheekiness, but also a look of penetration and an aura of melancholy. He had an instinctive depth of feeling, wariness and the hidden well of sadness of the true clown. He was a disarming man, quiet and effacing; a sad man, guileless and unpretentious. There was sweetness in his smile which was old, yet childlike.

Max had put aside his own ego and he became a good listener, interested in the lives of others. He was essentially a simple man. He talked of his parrot, of the joys of walking down Marine Parade, Brighton, in the winter when there were few people around. It pleased him to see old people enjoying themselves on a day trip.

Max's driving force was the desire to perform. He admitted : 'Off the stage I am nothing and only when I'm working in front of an audience can I come to life and become an interesting person.'

Max sat in a rickety chair in a tawdry dressing room. I asked him if he was going to use any new gags that evening. 'I tell you what, son. I'll try you out. If you laugh I'll slip the gag in tonight. I'll get 'em to put a spot on you—you'll be sitting in the front row—and you must laugh again, see?

'Now there's this woman who goes to the Motor Show. She was the sort who knew what she wanted. There it was, all big and shiny . . . the salesman, he was dead clever. He said, "Do you want a Baby Austin?" And she replied, "And how did you know my name was Austin? No," she said, "my husband's just bought a new Dodge." '

Encouraged by my reaction, Max tried out another one :

'There was this boy who had just come down from Oxford— that's the place where they have a school for illiterates. They learn to speak proper, like wot I does. He swore with every other word. It did upset his old man. He was a clergyman, see? "This is the house of God," 'e said. "Promise me that every time you swear you'll give the person nearest to you a sum of money." Next morning, the boy was going down the stairs when he tripped and fell over the mat. "Who put that bloody mat there?" he said. "I did," said the new maid. She was a nice bit of overtime an' all. Then the boy, 'e remembered his promise, fished in his pocket and all he had on 'im was his wallet. 'E 'ad to give the maid a quid. "Cor blimey," she said. "Like father, like son. Where do you want it, in the front room or up in the attic?" By the way, how did a poor struggling girl get a fur coat? She stopped struggling. And what's the difference between a girl getting out of a car and a rude joke? Sometimes you see it and sometimes you don't.'

When it came to the show Max addressed the house : 'I've got a pal of mine in the front row. I hope he's worth the five bob I've paid him. Make something of that, girl—filthy lot. No, listen. Put a spot on him. Now, you lot, 'ave a good look at 'im.' I was sitting barely three yards from Max and I experienced at first hand the genius of Miller because he told me the gags again and at the same time he told the entire audience. I laughed uncontrollably and the house laughed at me. 'I'm goin' to keep that in, lady. I'll keep it in, if you let me—for as long as you like, girl. You don't find good 'uns like that often, do you?'

Between houses I asked Max if he rationalised his humour. He told me it was totally instinctive.

'I don't know the reason for the success of my act. Experience helps. Schooling was no part of my life—it took me ten years of slogging. I suppose it was there, deep down. Timing is one of the secrets—how I deliver the telling lines. I don't rehearse cracking a gag. It's natural to me, like shelling an egg.

'I'm always on the look out for pockets of laughter. It might be the second row of the dress circle. I let 'em 'ave it next time, and blimey, the laughter, it spreads just like the measles.'

'You change your act continuously. You must be superbly confident?'

'Now, maybe, but it took twenty years to perfect my style. Different audiences; different circumstances—that was my way of learning my craft. I reckon I only reached my peak as an artist when I was in my mid-forties. Now I've got the know-how, I ride along, comfortable-like.

'In the 1930s I used to talk too quick, see? Even in films, people said they couldn't catch all I said. It came from being given an eight-minute spot on the halls, and trying to pack in as many gags as possible, I suppose. By 1940 I realised that if a joke was worth telling, it was worth telling well. I slowed down a bit and it paid off.

'I really enjoy making people laugh—I love my work—I must be in the right job, mustn't I? If I thought I was never going to work a theatre again, I would want to die.

'What I do is to sense the mood of every house. It's each new audience and their reactions to the jokes at the beginning of my act which tells me how far to go and what one I'm going to crack next. I never know till half way through one gag what the next one is going to be. I'm so tuned to my work, my mind somehow pulls out the story which is going to have the biggest follow-on impact. But I must have a free hand. I'm a solo turn, first, foremost and for ever. I don't want production, thank you. Nobody, not God Almighty, can tell me how to perform. I'm no good acting in a scripted show. That's why I've only been so-so on the radio and a dead loss on television. I won't change now, I'm too old, too set in the ways of stage work.'

'People are titivated by humour on the borderline of propriety—'

'Yes—that's my stock in trade. Sex is funny. It's the old story of if only we could see ourselves as others see us. It is an exciting thing for a boy fucking a girl. To the onlooker, it's as funny as a fat woman riding a ricketty donkey. When I go on about sex I've got ninety-five people in one hundred on my side. I don't use lavatory gags—I don't think to shit and to piss is funny; only necessary. My job is to keep an audience entertained, not to disgust them.

'It makes me sick to read some geezer was a train driver one day and a star the next. There never has been an overnight comic. Charlie Chaplin had years on the stage before he made it on films.

'I'm an original, but blimey, there have been imitators. There's one well-known comic—it wouldn't have been so bad if he was good at doing my act, but he wasn't—used to fluff the tag lines. I had a feud with another one too. He was the one who used to come in first house Monday, with his pencil and his notebook. But that's old hat now. When you get to my age, if you see trouble, walk round the corner. If all the trouble I've faced had started to get me down, I should have been dead the day before today.'

In a theatre, a signature tune can be a most poignant thing. When the reedy pit orchestra struck up with 'Mary From the Dairy' for Max Miller, the whole audience sat, on tenterhooks, waiting for him to appear. Occasionally he would delay his entrance. A foot bearing a correspondent's shoe and a leg with bright socks tucked beneath flowered plus-fours would be thrust out from behind the tabs. Everybody gasped. That was just what Max wanted. The house experienced a tingling in the pit of their stomachs. It was, somehow, an intensely moving experience when Max finally made his entrance to a roar of applause.

Max's stage make-up was as camp as any chorus boy from a 'twenties revue. Red for the lips, pink for the cheeks, and an abundance of eye shadow to show off those lovely blue optics. This steely suggestion of ambivalence was strong, and contradicted his image as the eternal chaser of those who wore the skirts. When Max cracked a real chestnut he would raise his hat as a token of respect, and reveal an obviously false hairpiece, which merged, uncomfortably, with the greying fringe round his cranium.

Max's act was a study in brilliant spontaneity. He started subtly, and each new gag induced a larger response. To quote Max, he was 'sensing the mood' and preparing the house for the plums to follow. Those early jokes were little more than quips, and in the hands of a lesser comedian, would have gone for nothing.

'I was on my way to the theatre tonight and a beautiful young lady stopped me. She said, "How do you do?" I said, "Do what?" and she said, "Please yourself." So we went in the park, just like the Babes in the Wood; 'cause, we knew more than the Babes. I said, "What do you do for a living?" and she said, "Yes." I said, "Let's *pause*, and look at the moon." She said, "You can keep your *paws* to yourself." '

Max looked funny, not because of his get-up, although this was an art in itself, but because of the way he wore it, as if it emanated from the wit and humour within him, which of course, it did. Without uttering a word, Max would place his hand on his left hip, smirk, wipe the smirk off his face, and stare, defiantly, at the audience.

'What if I am?' he'd say, and then, using the best camp walk in the business, he would move towards the backcloth and hang his overcoat on an invisible hook. 'I know what you're thinking, but you're wrong. Ain't I got a lovely figure, ducks? I say the funniest things too. I can't help it.'

Max had two famous props, a white book for the clean jokes and a blue one for the dirty ones. He pretended to consult them as he held a vast audience in the palm of his hand. Even when a gag was not particularly good, he buttonholed the audience in his own particular way, and persuaded them that 'It's all good stuff, lady.'

Max was a genius in the way he used silences. He'd sit on a tiny stool just behind the footlights, and pick up a guitar that had been left there for him. There would be a pause. He looked downwards. The audience followed his glance too. An enormous phallic symbol in the shape of a microphone thrust itself through a hole in the floor, and in an upward direction: 'Look at that, girl,' said Max. 'Must be the warm weather.' A woman in the gallery would go into hysterics. Max would wink at her through the din of hilarity. Simultaneously this communion between two people was shared by two thousand others:

> I like the girls who do
> I like the girls who don't.
> I hate the girl who says she will
> And then she says she won't.
> But the girl I like the best of all,
> And I think you'll say I'm right,
> Is the girl who says she never does
> But she looks as though she might.

'Gone dead quiet, hasn't it? It's the manager. He might go away, see?

'Spend half my life playing around, lady . . . we . . ll . . . I took this girl out—I took her the short cut—across the field—and I bent down and felt the grass. I said, "Some dew" and she said, "Some don't—good morning."

. 'There's a woman window cleaner down in Brighton—a woman . . . it's a man's job, 'in't it? There she was up a ladder. Five storeys up she was. They say it's unlucky to walk under a ladder—I took a chance. .

'I am a lad—hope so—we . . ll. Started courtin' when I was seventeen—honest—when I was seventeen. I was in the kitchen —I'll never forget it if I live that long—I was in the kitchen, brushing my hair back. I was puttin' on a clean collar—three inches high—the collar—looked as if I had my ears off.

'My mother said, "Where are you goin'?" I said, "I'm goin' courtin'." She said, "You're what?" I said, "I'm goin' courtin'." She said, "You're goin' to bed." Dead wicked. My mother— what a crafty woman, eh? She said, "Get up those stairs!" she said. "You're gettin' no supper—a piece of bread and butter— one slice."

'My father came in. "Where's Maxie?" "I caught him in the kitchen, making himself up. Going courtin'. I sent him to bed." He said, "What did you give him?"—"A piece of bread and butter." "Where's the frying pan?" She said, "You're not goin' to hit him with that, are you?"—"No—I'm going to fry him a piece of steak. You can't go courtin' on a piece of bread and butter?" Now listen . . .

'Haven't I got big eyes? Look—no, look . . . look . . . no . . . when I open 'em up . . . look . . . that's my mother's fault—look- ing all over England for my father—'ere—mind you, I only had two sweethearts in my life. That's enough, 'en it? Not a shame at all . . . straight on . . . butcher's hook . . . two sweethearts The first one was a telephone operator—the second one was a school teacher—not an ordinary teacher—Sunday school—they can't marry, you see They get a pension—listen—I stopped that—I gave her money instead. Listen. I took the first one out—right into the woods you see . . . ssh . . . not a soul about—very likely some gypsies passed. I started cuddlin' her—then, all of a sudden, she'd say, "Your three minutes are up."

'Now, the school teacher—entirely different—a smasher—a

tall girl with glasses—know what I did? No, listen! Do you know what I did? I breathed on 'em . . . honest. She couldn't see what I was doin'. Eventually I married her and had fifteen children . . . honest, that's the truth . . . too many? No, I don't know. It is, isn't it? And I told her, I said, "Any more, any more and I'll commit suicide." She said, "Don't be silly, Maxie!" "Listen," I said, "I'll commit suicide." I spoke to her proper.

'I came home a few months afterwards, I'd been away at sea, and she said, "It's happened again!" I said, "This is the end." I went upstairs, opened the drawer, got all my ties out, tied 'em all together fastened 'em round the gas mantle, got on the table, and was just about to jump off, when I said, "Don't be a mug, you might be hanging the wrong man."

'Got my own studio at Brighton, lady. A woman came to the door at seven-thirty one morning. She said, "Max, I want you to paint a snake on my knee." I went dead white—honestly . . . no . . . we . . ll. I'm not strong . . . I'm not strong . . . so, listen, I jumped out of bed, see—listen a minute! I started painting a snake just above her knee—that's where I started. But I had to chuck it in. She smacked me in the face—I didn't know a snake was that long . . . Well . . . how long is an ordinary snake?

'Met a girl the other day. I said, "You've got a nice figure," and she replied, "Yes, and I don't want you to spoil it." A change from the wife—she weighs twenty stone—that tells you what a lot I have to get through.'

With a deprecating hand Max admonished his audience for having lured him on to tell his funny tales. What George Robey's eyebrows did in the way of a silent rebuke, Max Miller, the subtle and brilliant comedian, suggested that if only he'd been allowed to finish his story, it would have turned out to be perfectly innocuous :

> 'When roses are red,
> They're ready for pluckin'
> When a girl is sixteen,
> She's ready for, 'ere, 'ere . . .'

'I was looking for digs, and this woman opened the door. "Yes?" she said, and I hadn't asked her. She said, "It'll be two pounds, all in, and I don't want children." She said, "I want what I want when I want it." I said, "You'll get what I've got when I've got it." She asked me to mind her baby that night. Did it howl! Gave it a dose of gin; got it to sleep, all right. When she got home, she said, "My, you are good with kids." "No," I replied, "I can't bear them." She'd got eight kids. Caught her one night stitching up her husband's pyjamas. "What's that for, girl?" "Well, a stitch in time saves nine." '

With a swivelling grin at his audience Max would say, 'You can't help liking him, can you?' A Cheeky Chappie had to be conceited. He also took full credit for things. 'I'm going to sing a song to you I've just written. You won't hear anybody else sing it. No one else dare sing it!' Who would dare sing about a "Fan Dancer Minus Her Fan"?'

Max stopped and addressed the gallery. 'Now then, none of that tittering up there—watch it, girl, you're the sort of woman who gets me a bad name. As I was saying, this girl suggested I might like to go up to her flat for coffee and games. I said, "You can cut out the coffee." We arrived and she said, "I didn't work as a stiffener in a laundry for nothing."

'Coo—what a boy—hope so; 'ere, listen, listen! We had a burglary in our street. I chased the burglar down the high street, past the fire station, past the butcher's, past the Co-op, eventually I caught him—by the cobblers.

' 'Ere, watch this, I'm going to dance now. All muscle, lady, every one working—all clever stuff, look, look. Both feet!

'Ever seen one of them, lady? 'ave you? You've seen one— well, he wanted a couple, girl, just like yours; so he 'ad two of 'em grafted on his back, see? He liked his vices versa:

'I don't like the girls who paint
Their cheeks just like a rose,
They may look what they ain't
With powder on their nose.

They're painting their toenails—
The thing that makes me vex
Is the way they're dressing,
They've got me guessing—
I wonder what they're going to paint next?

23

'Listen—this old lady—she left all her money to a brothel—she thought it was a soup kitchen. . . . Listen. I asked my dad. I said, "Dad—is it hard to please a woman?" He said, "It is if it isn't."

'A female rabbit—she was having a nibble—with a male rabbit. Eating grass, see? She got a bit coy, see. She said to the male rabbit. "Would you like a little family?" The male rabbit said, "That won't take us long, did it?"

'I took this girl home for a spot of pleasure. Didn't know I was kinky, did you? I told her to put her leather boots on, and got her to sit on the top of the chest of drawers. She said, "What now?" I said, "Put your arm out and turn the light on and off and after that pour that basin of water over your head." She got that bothered and she said, "When are we going to get down to a bit of the other?" I said, "What, in this weather?"

'This is clever stuff I'm giving you. Miller's the name, lady, there'll never be another, will there? They don't make 'em today, ducks. Boys will be boys, won't they? Lucky for you, girls, otherwise you'd get no fun . . . no . . . listen!

'I've got something new for you—it's called "A Fan Dancer Minus Her Fan"—that's like, without, see—"A Fan Dancer Minus Her Fan." I haven't finished it yet, haven't finished it, I'm working on it now. I've got the beginning, and I've got a part of the end, but what I'm after is the middle bit, that's what I want. If I get that, I'll be all right. I'll give you a rough idea of what it's all about. I'm not going to give you a lot, 'cos I shall want it when I come back, you see :

'I started courting a smashing fan dancer,
To marry her that was my plan;
Now it's all off with the smashing fan dancer,
She fell down and damaged her fan.

'And I want it to flow like that. I want it to flow like that—all the time, keep moving all the time. It's the middle bit, that's what I'm after, the middle bit. I shall get it, it'll come to me, I shall get it, might come to me about four o'clock in the morning, you don't know.

'Well, that's when I get inspiration, that's when I write all my stuff, you see. If it does, I shall be out of bed quick, you know. Oh yes, write it all down. Then the finish will be something like this, I'm not quite sure, but it'll be something like this :

'Alas, that poor girl, she's gone home to her mother,
Till her fan is mended or she gets another.

'Then you all come in with "Oh dear, what can the matter be." It'll be all right when I've finished with it, won't it, lady?'

Max stopped suddenly and moved stealthily towards the wings and looked around. He seemed satisfied, but then he paused, before moving on tiptoes towards the footlights.

'Has he gone?'

Voices from the back of the auditorium shouted back, 'Who, Max?'

'The manager.'

'Yes.'

'Well, I'll start on the blue book in a moment. Well, this blonde obviously took a fancy to me. She said she worked in a chemist's shop until she let the *pharm—a—see*. Now she's got a job in a photographer's shop. I said, "You look well developed." Of course, I shouldn't talk about the women like this. I'm a happily married man and I'm proud. It's too late to be otherwise.

'My wife had to move her seat in the cinema three times yesterday. I said, "Were you molested?" and she said, "Yes—eventually." I went home the other night—now there's a funny thing. I said, "Hello, mother of three." And she said, "Hello, father of two." I said, "How did you get those two black eyes?" She answered, "The lodger gave them to me." I went straight up to that lodger : "Did you give my wife two black eyes?" "Yes," he said, "she's been unfaithful to us."

Max Miller's complex stories were, in effect, a string of preparatory jokes, some of which were almost like something casually dropped in, leaving the audience hardly believing what they had heard. Max would then, gradually and relentlessly, increase the pressure to a hilarious conclusion. A wicked smile signalled the impending pay-off seconds before it arrived. Once the shaft was delivered, he would stand back with a cheeky grin, and observe the accuracy of his aim.

The roar of laughter from the audience comprised a release of tension on their part, pleasurable surprise at the outcome, linked with genuine amusement. Max never let a laugh die. Just as it was ebbing away, he would whip in a new line, thus sustaining the enjoyment. On paper, a graph of the volume of laughter he induced, and its subsequent decline into silence, represented an upturned V. A typical example of this sort of joke started as a casual aside :

'I met a pal of mine called Harry. I said, "Hello, Harry—I hear you are married."

' "Yes."

' "Well, now you are married you know what's what." (LAUGH)

' "What?"

' "Now you're married you must know what's what."

' "I don't know what you mean."

'Harry, all the way home—"Now I'm married, now I know what's what—I can't understand it."

'He got indoors, climbed the stairs, went into the bedroom. (LAUGH) There was his wife, happy and expectant. (LAUGH) He took all his clothes off. (LAUGH) Turned out the light. (LAUGH) Didn't want to get out again, see? (LAUGH) There was Harry, fumbling about in the dark. (LAUGH) Suddenly, he put his hand out about a foot in front of him. (ROAR) Harry said, "What's that?" (ROAR) and the wife said, "What's what?" ' (TERRIFIC ROAR)—and as it subsided Max jumped in with : 'And there it was, on the mantelpiece, all the time.' (LAUGH)

Occasionally a woman would laugh in the wrong place. Max, displaying an expert and infallible exercise in technique, would slip in an aside like, 'What's that you've got up yer jumper, girl, a roll top desk?' Then, miraculously, he picked up the main joke again and continued to the climax, by which time the laughter was totally uncontrolled, and occasionally reached the pitch of hysteria. Then Max realised the house was exhausted; it had reached saturation point. He would introduce a song which he put across in an appealing, lilting voice. He had a wide repertoire. Sentimental ones included 'My Old Mum' and 'On a Sunday Afternoon'. There were romantic ballads : 'Voulez Vous Promenade, ma Chérie' or humorous ones, 'I'm One of Nature's Greatest Gifts To Women'. Max usually concluded his act with a number and a favourite of his was 'Isn't It Grand to See Someone Smile?' There would be call after call, before Max disappeared into the wings, leaving the audience wanting more. A great night in the theatre was over.

Occasionally on a first house, Monday, the reaction would be slow. On one of his many appearances at the Empress, Brixton, Max walked off the stage, strolled behind the skycloth, exchanged a few words with me, and then re-entered on the opposite prompt side. The stage was empty for a least seventy seconds, and it seemed like an eternity. The audience sat there thunderstruck and as silent as a grave. No other artist would have taken such a risk. Max Miller had complete control over an audience's reactions. His opening gambit was :

'I'm back—just to make you appreciate me all the more. Haven't I got lovely blue eyes, lady?' Max deprecated the lack of seriousness with a wave of the hand—'No! No! When I open 'em up?' and he ogled them anxiously. 'Do you fancy me, girl? You do? Well, you've got good taste.'

No wonder Max Miller, 'The Cheeky Chappie', was described as 'The Pure Gold of the Music Hall'. He knew everything about performing in that unique institution : laughter was his business.

3   Early Years 1894–1919

MAX MILLER WAS born in Brighton. Apart from service in the First World War and when he was on tour, it remained his home throughout his life and he had a great love for the place.

In the 1890s Brighton had seen better days. As late as 1906 the *Daily Mail* published a front-page article on the town in which Brighton was condemned as an unenterprising, unattractive and outdated holiday resort. This was not wholly fair. Harry Preston, who took a tenure of the Royal York Hotel in 1901, was a dynamic individual who helped spur the town to a new prosperity.

In the year of Max Miller's birth the Palace Pier was completed and in 1901 a theatre added. There was an atmosphere of raffish gaiety quite different from that of the West Pier, which was regarded as more select. It was around the supports of the newly-built Palace Pier that Max played and first watched a concert party. That spurred him on to form his own alfresco entertainment called The Beachcombers. The entertainment was good enough for people to throw pennies and so it was far removed from childish exhibitionism. He sang this song :

> 'He stood on the corner
> His tongue hanging out
> His hands in his pocket
> His shirt hanging out
> How I love him

I can't forget him
Wherever he goes.'

Brighton was a town of some size for a seaside resort. In 1900 it had a population of around 120,000. There was much unemployment and social unrest. As in other communities the poor resorted to public charity, the soup kitchens and the parson. There was also begging from the wealthy and sympathetic visitors to the town. Max Miller's family availed themselves of all these benefits.

An extraordinary aspect of Brighton life was the activities of bird catchers. A number of families specialised in this trade. Every morning in the season some twenty or thirty men went from Brighton onto the Downs where they set nets to catch birds of all kinds. Larks and wheatears were sold as delicacies to the big hotels. Singing birds were kept alive and sold in cages. Sparrows and starlings were plucked and sold by the plateful as they still are on the Continent today. Rare species of birds were sold for as much as ten shillings or a sovereign to private collectors.

Nellie Parsons, who was a year older than Max and knew him in his childhood, said : 'Max was very clever at earning a few pennies. He soon learnt about bird catching on the Downs and he used to go to Brighton station with the birds and sell them to visitors on their way home to London.'

Percy Sargent, Max's younger brother, also remembers Max's youthful business activities.

'He loved his mother, and whatever he got from doing odd jobs, he always shared it with her. He'd go round the streets with a bucket, picking up the horse manure which he used to flog to the rich folk in Hove. He was very artful with the way he made nets out of old and discarded fish nets and he used them to catch birds. When he was caddying he would pinch golf balls and sell 'em the next day.'

Edwardian Brighton owed its new prosperity greatly to Harry Preston. His genial personality and enthusiasm for yachting, motoring, flying and the theatre brought about a renewal of the town's importance as a centre for sporting and stage people. The greatest single influence in the rebirth of Brighton's success was the growing popularity of the motor car. In 1905 Preston promoted a scheme to have a tarmac surface made on Madeira Drive from the Palace Pier to Kemp Town, a distance of nearly a mile, to enable it to serve from time to time as a race track.

From his youth Max loved motor cars; he was only fifteen when he learned to drive and he was probably influenced by the early vogue in Brighton for 'the rush and roar of motor drawn traffic'.

Owing to Edward VII's friendship with the Sassoons, and his desire to visit his daughter, Royal patronage gave another fillip to the town. The King arrived in 1908. His visit was marred by a demonstration of unemployed outside the mansion in which he was staying.

The Brighton Herald remarked on the affray :

'The King is declared to be deriving both health and enjoyment from his holiday; and this fact, and the fact he has been rejoicing in floods of sunshine is being chronicled in the press all the country over . . . The success of the King's visit will do more to aid employment than would be effected by any number of socialistic demonstrations. The man who will militate against the success of the visit is an enemy of this town.'

Clearly the King had been annoyed by the curious crowds who would fill the seats of Marine Parade waiting for him to appear. Next year the chief constable, Sir William Gentle, solved the question of the King's privacy in a clever way. He enlisted the help of the borough surveyor and all the seats where the spectators placed themselves were given a coat of fresh bright green paint every morning.

During one of his visits the King attended the police gymnasium in two of the arches in the lower promenade where poor children were fitted with clothing provided out of a fund established by Sir William Gentle. Percy Sargent told me his family took charity from this source.

Max Miller was born Thomas Henry Sargent on 21st November 1894 at 43 Hereford Street, Brighton, the son of James Sargent, a builder's labourer, and Alice Sargent née West.

Max fabricated so much about his life that it is hard to establish fact from fiction. He claimed to have been born in London in 1891 and to have moved to Brighton at the age of three. In fact he was born four years later in Brighton. This is probably the only time in history that an actor has made himself out to be older than he really was. He also said he was fifth in a family of twelve living in a four-roomed house near Brighton station. In fact he was second in a family of five, having one older sister Florence, two younger brothers, Jimmy and Percy, and a younger sister, Elsie. As to a home they never had one since they were continuously on the move.

Max, talking about his early life, although admitting great hardship : 'It may seem a bit of a joke to you, but it hasn't been a joke to me,' added a lot of embroidery. He claimed to have worked as a barrow boy with his father in the Caledonian Market; he said he ran away to sea; he said he started his show-business career in a circus. All this was nonsense.

The nearest he got to working in a circus was cleaning the animal cages for one week at a travelling circus which called at Brighton. He worked as a general labourer for Rowland's fair on the site of Tilling's bus garage in Hove.

Many people thought Max was Jewish and he did not discourage them in this belief. Indeed he thought it would help him in his theatrical career where the Jewish fraternity held key positions. His stage name, which his wife chose in 1921, had Jewish connotations. His father was of Romany stock, though Percy Sargent, Max's brother, derisively called him a didicoy.

'My father's brother was a busker. He worked a pitch in Bognor playing on a one-string fiddle and an accordion. Dad had a sense of wanderlust too which is a characteristic of didicoys—that was possibly why he never stayed in any job for too long. He was a real fighter and that's why he often got the push. Dad was a boilermaker and he worked on the railways too. For a time he did some construction work on Shoreham Harbour and Max did odd labouring jobs there too. Like most fighting men, Dad had a taste for the bottle. He frequented the poorest and roughest pubs in the area and he sang for his beer; his great haunt was the Cliftonville Hotel, outside Hove station. The public bar there was called "The Blood Hole", because of the blood spilt there in various brawls. My mother had a tough time. She died in the Spanish 'flu epidemic.'

Thus Max was brought up in uncertain circumstances and many times the family faced a serious crisis, as Percy Sargent recalled. 'When things got very bad for us we went to bed with empty bellies. When the rent was due we moved; from Shoreham to Portslade to Hove to Brighton and back again. We always kept an old pushcart available to carry our belongings and a bench that was long enough to seat us all. When the digs only had two beds, we kids shared one, with me and my brothers, Jimmy and Max, one end, and the girls the other. Mum and Dad had the other one. Sometimes, if we were overdue with the rent, the landlord would take the windows out to make us pay up.

'Dad would run up as big a bill for rent as possible and when the landlord started to threaten him, we'd do a midnight flit. Out with the old barrow and we usually made for under the pier where we'd camp out until we could get fixed up with a new flat the next day.'

When Max Miller was a star, a young reporter, unaware of his background, asked him if his childhood experiences had helped to develop his talent as a comedian.

'My talent as a comedian is a gift of God,' was his reply.

Nellie Parsons remembers Max when he was six. 'He was a nice looking boy, big for his age, fresh and cheeky. He was always up to mischief and he seemed to see the saucy side of things. He made much of himself; as if he was somebody. That's why he got the nickname of "Swanky Sargent". The strange thing was, Harry, as we called him then, had nothing to boast about. He looked a proper rag bag. Because he was tall, his get-ups made him stand out even more.

'I can see Harry now, wearing somebody's old cast-off boots, his arse hanging out of his trousers, and a gent's coat on him, which was cut down to size. Even if his shirt was an old one, he always wore a clean paper collar, and if he hadn't got a tie, he'd wear a bootlace instead. I remember he once went to the school in Ellen Street, Hove, with his mother's shoes on. Again, when he was a pupil of the school in Elm Grove, it was summer time, and he arrived barefooted. The teacher found him an old pair

33

of slippers which were too big for him, so she tied them on his feet with string. For the time they were there, the Sargents were the roughest family in Goldstone Street.

'He used to play at the side of the railway with my brother and other boys who lived in our street. My mother used to be sorry for him. She often gave Harry an evening meal. She used to stew up bones to make soup. Afterwards Harry would play cards with the others and he nearly always won and he would jump up and down with excitement. Their game was banker and Harry was so quick—we used to think he cheated, but nobody could be quite sure, he was smart, you see.

'Harry's mother was a hard-working woman and for a time she was a flower seller. His father was a bit of a bruiser. Although the Sargents were always doing midnight flits, Harry would come back for that cup of soup and that game of cards. He loved to lark about and have fun—more than the other boys. He kidded himself he could dance, and I used to see him practising his steps under the West Pier.'

Max never went to any school for long, nor was his attendance regular. He left school, barely literate, at twelve. Max could read but he was never able to write properly. In later life when he thought up a gag he would get someone to write it down for him, in particular his wife, who managed his affairs.

Whenever Max described his youthful experiences, the elements were true, but being 'The Cheeky Chappie' he couldn't resist bringing in some music-hall hyperbole.

'The teacher used to say, "Come out, Sargent! Lie across that desk!" Then I had the usual strokes. One afternoon, the teacher called me out six times. After she'd finished I said, "I think I'll stay here."

' "Why?" she asked.

' "I won't be able to sit down now," I told her.

'That time she had to laugh too. It's a funny thing, but forty years later, when I played the Brighton Hippodrome, she came to see me in my dressing room.

' "You used to be a dunce at school," she said. "But you haven't turned out to be much of a dunce after all."

'Then she told me she'd never seen me on the stage. That was worse than any beating she gave me.

'I left school when I was twelve because my parents needed a
bit of money brought into the home. My first job was as a milk
boy at three shillings a week and commission. When I was
delivering the milk I used to drink some out of a dozen bottles
and fill up the rest with water. I was taking an interest in my
work, see? I wanted to get rich quick and have a dairy of my
own.

'One day the boss called me in and said, "Sargent, I've got a
surprise for you."

'I could hardly wait to ask him what it was.

' "You finish on Saturday," he said.

' "Finish? Why?"

' "The customers have been complaining about the milk."

' "Oh. Too much cream?" I said, trying to make him laugh.

' "You mean too much water."

' "Well, rain water never hurt anybody."

' "Rain water?" he said. "Blimey, one woman complained
about a tiddler in her milk."

'When Saturday came I took my wages and commission,
three pennies, and went home. I found my father eating
shepherd's pie in the kitchen. I could see he wasn't feeling too
good so I stepped in quick and said, "Dad, I've got the sack. It
wasn't my fault, we ran out of milk."

' "Ran out of milk?"

'I told him the truth and it hurts to think what happened then.

'My next job was in a fish and chip shop in George Street,
Hove. I often get a laugh when I pass it now. I got two-and-six
a week and a fish supper every night. I used to take the supper
home and share it with my family.

'I had to get up at an hour so early you wouldn't believe there
was such a time of day. I had to go to the Brighton fish market.
In those days for a bob you could buy enough to feed three or
four families. When I got back to the shop I had to peel the
spuds and serve from behind the counter.

'I was very capable at the counter, never giving overweight
with the chips. One day an old lady came in for a tuppeny piece
of fish and a pennorth of chips. I sprinkled on the vinegar and
handed them over. A little while later she came back and pushed
the bag across the counter.

' "No salt!" she said.

'I could hardly believe my ears and yelled "What!"

' "No salt!" she said.

' "Blimey!" I said. "At first I thought you said, 'One short.' "

'The guvnor was standing there and he laughed like anything. "You're a smart lad. How would you like to go to the fish market by yourself tomorrow?"

' "You mean I can go and buy all the fish myself!"

' "If you like."

'I couldn't clear up the shop quickly enough that night. I rushed home to tell my father the good news. As usual he was sitting in the kitchen eating, you've guessed it, shepherd's pie. I told him what had happened and then I said, "I want you to practise with me so that I'll be good at the auction tomorrow morning."

' "All right, but what do I have to do?" said Dad.

' "You'll be the auctioneer, and I'll be the buyer."

'Dad did as he was told but he was too slow and so he said, "Let's switch over, you be the auctioneer." Did I show him! I rattled off all I'd learnt from the market auctioneers and Dad was flabbergasted. He just sat back and stared at me and when it was over he said,

' "I never met a kid who could talk so fast and so much. Blimey—look, it's three o'clock."

'When I realised I had only two hours sleep ahead of me, I went to bed with my boots on. Next morning I pushed the barrow to Brighton fish market which used to function from boats landed on the beach. I successfully bid for a fine lot of fish.

'On the way to the shop a brewer's dray came round the corner, smashed into the barrow and spilled the lot. While I was standing there, trying not to cry, a lot of people came out of houses nearby to see what the crash was. They helped me to pick up the barrow and helped themselves to the fish.

'When I got back to the shop the guv'nor looked at my little lot and said, "How much did you pay for these?" When I told him, he said, "You've been robbed. I'll see about this in the morning when I go to the market."

'Well, I was too proud of my business ability to let him think I couldn't buy fish so I told him about the accident.'

Max never stuck at a job for long but drifted as his fancy took him. For a short time he worked for a tailor.

'All I did all day was to sew on buttons, thread needles, and pick pins up off the floor.'

At last Max found something to suit him—caddying on Brighton and Hove golf course. There he came across monied people. Their style obviously influenced him and at the same time he was able to exercise his wit and his facility for making a bob on the side by selling 'lost' golf balls the next day. He was paid one shilling and sixpence a round of which he had to give threepence to the caddie master. He usually did two rounds a day but more on Sundays. If it rained he got nothing at all.

'Even in those days I was always trying to make people laugh. One bloke I was caddying for said to me, "What do you think of golf?"

' "Me?" I answered. "I think it's a good walk spoilt."

'He laughed and said, "If you go on like that you'll be a comedian some day." He was the only one who ever said that to me.

'Every evening, about five of us caddies used to stop in the bushes on the way home and play banker. I used to win pretty often, and whenever I won anything I'd go back and put it in my money box.

'On Saturday nights some of us would buy twopence worth of coal and put it in a brazier and take it up into a bunker. We'd play cards till we got tired and then we'd sleep there all night. We did this so that we could be at the club house early on Sunday mornings—that was the day a lot more caddies turned up and if you weren't there early you'd find yourself at the end of a queue of fourteen or fifteen.

'Sometimes a golfer would say to me, "I've got a pair of shoes that might be of use to you, what size do you take?"

'I didn't dare tell him my size in case it wouldn't be the right one, and then he might say, "Sorry, they might not fit." So I used to look at his feet and say, "They'd fit me all right." I'd be told to go to a certain address and get them. So I'd go and a maid would hand over the shoes. Just to show him I'd got the shoes, I'd go round with him wearing the shoes just once—even if it crippled me. Then I'd sell 'em and put the dough in my money box.'

Max always had his ear to the ground and when a lady talked to him on the golf course and told him he was wasting his time there he listened to her advice. She suggested he might become a chauffeur and he jumped at the opportunity. She got him a job in London with a Bond Street motor firm and gave him sufficient money for a hair cut and clothes.

'I was never taught to drive a car. I just had to clean them and help repair them. One day one of the blokes thought he might teach me to drive, so he took me out and put me at the wheel. I ran into a lamp-post and got the sack. Then I went back to Brighton. I learnt to drive eventually and I used to be a chauffeur at the Royal Hotel.

'Even in those days I had ideas of singing and telling stories for my living. I used to go into the pubs at night where they had somebody playing the piano, and I sang the popular comic songs. When anybody put a few pennies in the box marked, "Give generously to the pianist" I was given something for myself. But I was never really stage struck.'

Albert J Baker, a Brightonian, knew Max from 1910 until his death fifty-three years later.

'Max would go round the pubs with his father doing an impromptu act. The father was a tough old boot who used to play the piano whilst Max would sing and then tell a few near-the-knuckle jokes. When they played "The Blood Hole" in Hove the pub was never short of patrons. They also appeared at "The Half Moon" in West Street.'

It was worthwhile for a poor man to join the Territorials. He had to attend the drill hall regularly and go to an annual camp. It was a release from humdrum life and there was a sense of camaraderie. A childhood friend of Max was Edward Bernardi; he advised Max to join the Sussex Territorials.

'I got to know Max Miller in 1910. He was using his real name of Harry Sargent then of course. He was just an ordinary bloke; nobody even considered he'd make much of his life, let alone become a stage star.

'His family was in poor circumstances. Harry used to walk

about with an overcoat on in the summer because the backside of his trousers was falling out and he was wearing somebody's discarded dicky instead of a shirt. Even so Harry always sported a pair of spats he'd dug out of a nob's dustbin—that's why we called him "Swank"—"Swanky Sargent." He was a nice looking fellow—and his cheery personality diverted one's attention from the fact he was dressed in rags.

'Six of us youngsters used to go around together as a sort of gang. Max was the leader, not because he was particularly out-standing, I think it was that he had a ready answer for anybody. He was mighty quick on the uptake, especially when he played Crown and Anchor. Another favourite game of ours was banker and Harry showed himself up as a bit of a card sharper.

'He got the loan of a motorbike—from where I can't imagine because they were few and far between in those days. We were on one of the Territorial camps outside Margate and Max said one night, "How about going into Ramsgate for the evening?" I thought it would be a good idea and so off we went. Well, on the journey back, we ran out of petrol. Suddenly we heard a car approaching. Harry said, "Quick—make yourself scarce!" He waved down this car and said, "I'm carrying important dis-patches. It's essential I get to my destination. Can you give me some petrol?" The driver gave Max a whole tin of petrol. We filled up and went on our way.

'Our gang were all members of the same unit in the Terri-torials. We only signed for home defence. When war was declared in 1914 we didn't want to split up. We all decided to volunteer together for overseas duties.'

Another Brightonian, E L Coles, wrote to tell me he attended the recruiting office in Marmion Road, Hove.

'In front of me in the queue was a young man who was addressed by the recruiting sergeant :

' "Your name?"

' "Sargent, sergeant," said the recruit.

' "Are you trying to be funny? I asked you what is your name."

' "Harry—Sargent."

' "What's your surname, you idiot?"

' "Sargent, Sergeant."

'Everybody in that room was reduced to fits of laughter and it was only then that the recruiting sergeant understood there could be somebody called Harry Sargent.'

Max took up the story with his posting to Mhow in central India. 'They taught me to be a rough rider. I was one of the founders of a concert party at Mhow and we called ourselves The Lightners.

'I took all the women's parts so I was always going to the captain and saying, "How are the horses?" You see, when one of the horses died I used to get their tails and make them into wigs.

'Later on we were sent to Delhi, where malaria got me down. When I was better they made me a corporal and got me driving a hospital van. I was going along a street in Delhi one evening when I saw a lovely white girl. That was very unusual so I thought I'd chat her up.

'I pulled alongside and asked her the way to the hospital—which I knew. When she told me I kidded I couldn't follow her directions. So she got in beside me and showed me the way. We got very friendly. I found out she was the wife of a school teacher. I arranged to meet her the next day when she introduced me to her father and mother.

'She used to ask me to visit her at home, but never when her husband was there. One day when we were sitting in the drawing room a man walked in. "My husband," she said, and introduced us.

'He pulled out a revolver. "What's that for?" I asked him rather nervously.

' "Practice," he told me. "I'm considered a very good shot. Come out into the garden."

'So we went into the garden, and he started knocking bottles off the top of a wall. I left pretty soon, and I didn't see the girl or her husband after that.

'One evening I went to a dance and stayed out all night. It happened the hospital wanted me that night to drive to an urgent case. When I got back I had to go before the Major, who gave me seven days' pack drill. He put me under a sergeant who was a friend of mine. He said, "I wouldn't carry that heavy pack around if I were you. Fill it up with paper."

40

'When the officer made his inspection he found my pack full of paper and I got another seven days!'

Throughout Max Miller's career stories circulated about his meanness. However, he was always generous to blind people and during the Second World War he offered his large house at Ovingdean, near Brighton, to St Dunstan's—an offer which was gratefully accepted. Max Miller's sympathy for the blind originated during his service in Mesopotamia in 1915. He remembered one incident.

'Well, we'd been up in the front line—or as near to it as we gunners could get—and a shell went off a few yards away. I wasn't hit; but the blast knocked me out. For three days I was completely blind. It was a nightmare, but I've never forgotten anything that was done to get my sight back. Then, during the last war, I made sure I was able to repay the use of my big blue eyes by donating my house to St Dunstan's.'

Edward Bernardi remembered The Lightners concert party at Mhow.

'I was the pianist and I also arranged the numbers which were all in the piano key, and I transposed them for the various instruments.

'Apart from his odd engagements in pubs in and around Brighton, this show gave Max Miller his first real experience as an entertainer. He used to sing, dance a few steps, and tell some rather smutty stories. You had to be good to please the troops, but Max was nothing exceptional in those days. He was a rattling good female impersonator; in my opinion, even then, using teased-out hair from horses' tails for wigs and costumes borrowed from the natives, he beat Danny La Rue.

'We didn't get many concessions, except to escape guard duty now and then. Max was always a bit of a rebel, and when he got lippy with the NCOs he was up for the high jump.

'We were all posted to Mesopotamia in 1915. It was a terrible place and more men were lost through illness than from bullets from the enemy. We returned to India in 1916 but from 1917 until the end of the war we were in Mesopotamia.'

Mr Mountain also served with Max Miller in India and Mesopotamia. He was known as 'Ginger' to his mates. He also appeared in the concert party The Lightners.

'I shall never forget Max walking through the streets of Delhi dressed as a woman for his appearance in the show. He got some very rude remarks thrown at him!

'Max was known as "Swanky Sargent" to everybody. He was a lad—very friendly and a good sport. Mind you, I learnt not to play him at cards. He waited till payday and then he made a bit more at cards. I got caught on board. We sailed on 29th September 1914 and a game of banker with Harry lost me more than I could afford. But there were no hard feelings. I knew he'd had a rough time as a kid and I'd seen him selling newspapers to make a few pennies on the street corners of Brighton.

'Things were terrible in Mesopotamia. A man called Short shouted out, "I've been bitten by a viper!" He hadn't—a bullet had gone clean through his calf. It was boiling hot in the day and bitterly cold at night.'

After demobilisation Max headed for Brighton—as usual the family had been on the move but he soon found their new *temporary* abode. Percy Sargent was there when he arrived.

'I heard a shout. I opened the door and there was Max getting out of a two-horse trap. He looked none the worse for his war service. That night he said, "I'm going to get dressed up, Percy." He did—in an officer's uniform he'd got hold of somehow; there were two pips up, I remember. He went off to the Brighton Hippodrome and mixed with real officers in the bar—that took a bit of acting on his part, but being Max he got away with it.

'He told Dad that he'd enjoyed working in an amateur concert party when he was in the army and he was determined to go on the professional stage and, what's more, get to the top. "Give it a try, son," was Dad's reply.'

4 Concert Party 1919–1921

IN THE YEAR 1919 Harry Sargent was twenty-six years of age. It was three years before Max Miller's name appeared on bills of variety.

After the rigours of four years' active service overseas he returned to England with some polish and a determination to succeed in life. Up to the outbreak of the First World War Max hardly left Brighton, except for annual camps with the Territorials and a short stay in London as a motor mechanic. He realised that a successful future lay in the big city.

Max knew little about the theatrical profession except that agents had offices in and around Charing Cross Road. He arrived at Victoria and caught a tram to Brixton where he found lodgings in Kennington Road for twelve shillings a week. The next day he went 'Up West' and walked down Prosser's Lane* and he was dismayed by what he saw. Dozens of good acts, with years of experience, were to be seen hanging around at street corners, waiting for agents' runners to find them and fix up an engagement. The chances for an unknown, with only amateur experience, to gain a foothold on the professional stage, seemed very slight.

That year was a lean one for variety artists. The halls were beginning to capitulate to the cinema, which had captured popular patronage throughout the country. Speciality acts were

---

* The profession's name for Charing Cross Road where prossing or cadging loans was prevalent.

still in demand, but they had to be outstanding. A superb exponent of sleight of hand, or a dancer with amazing agility and twinkling toes, could get a string of contracts with the major circuits.

Max's experience with a rough and ready concert party had been of some use to him. He could claim to be a comedian of sorts. Methods of trial and error had taught him to be selective in his use of material and he knew the limitations in his talent as a patter merchant and a vocalist.

There were several types of comedian : character, eccentric and light. A character comic impersonated a readily recognisable type; it could have been a blundering Bobby as played by Charlie Austin, a shabby man of the people such as Scott Sanders portrayed or the irascible schoolmaster of Will Hay. An eccentric comedian traded on physical peculiarity like the diminutive Little Tich, whose gallery of portraits included a passionate senora; or he made himself up as a very strange personage with a red nose and idiotic clothes, as for example T E Dunville. A light comedian was well dressed, looked as handsome as possible, and usually sang and danced in between inconsequential patter. Nearly every artist in this category who was working in 1919 modelled himself on the dashing and immaculate Fred Barnes.

Max Miller's personality was strong enough in itself to hold an audience. There was no need to hide his own identity behind a mask of eccentricity. He scanned the professional press and saw there was a singing and dancing competition to be held at the London, Shoreditch, a famous theatre of variety in the East End. There was a prize of six pounds and a week's engagement. Max recalled the episode.

'An old bloke got first prize and I came second. But the old 'un was not up to doing a twice-nightly engagement for a week, so I got the job. On the Thursday the manager came up to me and said, "Harry, is it true that you're walking here every day all the way from the Kennington Road, Brixton?" I said, "Yes—I can't afford the fare." He gave me a pound and said, "Don't walk any more." Some years later I was top of the bill at that theatre, getting forty pounds a week, and I gave the manager back his quid. He said he'd get it framed.

'After that I couldn't find any more work in London, so I

went back to Brighton and I spotted an advert in the local paper for artists to appear in Jack Sheppard's concert party on the Madeira Lawns, Madeira Drive, Kemp Town. I applied and got the engagement as a light comedian. The pay was three-pounds five a week.'

Max's wife, Kathleen Marsh, was also engaged for that summer season. She remembered her first day's rehearsal early in May 1919.

'I was on a bus. I was on my way to the rehearsal. Sitting opposite me was a chap wearing a pink shirt. As I sat looking at that shirt I thought to myself, "How horrible!" When I got off the bus I had a terrible feeling that this man was following me. I got to the door of the rehearsal hall and forgot about him. Then suddenly I saw him. It was Max, then known as Harry Sargent, going for an audition for Mr Sheppard. He got the job, and two years later we were married.'

Max Miller was one of dozens of top-line artists who owed their start in the profession to seaside entertainments. Concert parties had their beginning in the mid-nineteenth century when railways brought the common people to the beaches. In the true tradition of strolling players, artists 'without a shop,' meaning without an engagement in a theatre, often resorted to alfresco work. This meant playing to passers-by in the open air. They took their shows to the public.

Sometimes these itinerant actors played solo, especially experts on the harp, but more generally they formed themselves into groups, and by the 1880s nigger minstrels were very popular at most seaside resorts.

The pierrot was once a character in the harlequinade which was part of a pantomime. In the 1890s Clifford Essex formed a company of pierrots and soon similar combinations were challenging minstrels for the public's favour. Pierrots and minstrels began to fade in popularity by 1914, and modern-dress concert parties, which were already well established, took their place.

Primitive concert parties stopped off at any convenient spot, the better established ones played on recognised pitches. Their backcloth was the sea, the auditorium, the pebbles on the beach. The artists improvised in the true commedia dell' arte tradition. Their minds had become a storehouse for quips and songs, and

they were adept in bringing out the right material to hold stragglers for sufficient time for their bottler or collector to squeeze
out the pennies. Jack Sheppard prolonged this tradition till the
1930s.

Max Miller's engagement with Jack Sheppard taught him all
the elements of his craft, which he later polished to perfection.
The show was well rehearsed and every artist had to have a
talent for solo work. Concert parties gave the toughest lesson in
salesmanship, projection and the hardening of personality. A
theatre held a captive audience, but the open air had no such
security. The people passed by; to make them stop, listen and be
held, needed a magnetic force. As Max once said of his early
days in concert parties, 'It wasn't a question of mind over matter,
but of mind over Maxie.'

The artist gave everything. It was poignant to see the song
and dance man tapping his heart out on those creaking boards,
his forehead trickling with sweat on a hot summer's day. One
foot wrong felt like the kiss of death—a scowl came from the
pianist which preceded the departing figures of onlookers.

The essence of the appeal of concert party entertainment was
the bond between the player and the audience. The concerted
numbers, featuring the whole cast, were executed with extravagant flair, and gave compulsion for everybody to join in the
popular choruses of the day.

Two concert parties had a tremendous success on the West
End stage—H G Pelissier's The Follies in Edwardian times, and
The Co-optimists in the 1920s.

In 1919 Brighton was approaching its heyday. The passage
from Old Steine to the Palace Pier had become a frantic bustle
of crowds and traffic. Every day Max had to dodge between
motorbikes and charabancs, on his way to Madeira Drive and
the open-air theatre of Jack Sheppard.

Everywhere stood queues; for the two piers, for buses, for
trams and for Volk's Electric Railway which ran along the
beach.

The War was over and for the first time in four years people
could afford a holiday and relax again. Furthermore, the advent
of the motorcar and the charabanc brought the arrival of the
day trippers, many of whom had never left London before. The

beaches were black with families—dad in his shirtsleeves and braces, mum clutching the sandwiches and a bottle of milk, and their kids with buckets and spades and sticks of Brighton rock.

Max welcomed the return of the sun, the sparkle of the waves, the sound of the bands, the colour of the flags. He even had a welcome for the motor-stirred-up dust and the smell of petrol. For together they meant fine weather, peace after a bloody war, and patrons with pennies clasped in hot hands and readily dropped into his bottle, and, after a share-out with the other artists, into his pocket.

Jack Sheppard remembered Max in those early days.

'Directly I saw him at that audition I was impressed by his appearance. Tall and good looking; I wasn't put off by his shabby clothes. His personality captured me from the start. He did a song and dance, and he seemed to be quite good, so I engaged him at two pounds ten—not the three pounds five as advertised—he had no experience to speak of. I said, "I'll make up your money, Mr Sargent, if you prove your worth during the season." His wife-to-be was in the company, Kathleen Marsh— she had a nice contralto voice.

'Max, or Harry Sargent as he was known then, was essentially a song and dance man. The first number he ever sang with me was "Give Me The Moonlight, Give Me The Girl." The other song he put over well was "What Could Be Sweeter than That?"

'He progressed slowly but surely, gaining in confidence and playing out to the audience. Playing in the open air is tough— you have to be strong enough to hold the stragglers outside the enclosure—it was those extra pennies that made up our salaries. I will say when Max wasn't performing, but bottling, few people escaped without giving something.'

Jack Sheppard, whose real name was Frank Gomm, arrived in Brighton in the summer of 1903 when he set up an alfresco concert party on the beach. He later established a group called The Highwaymen, and it was then he chose the stage name of Jack Sheppard inspired by the legendary character who broke out of prisons. Among the other artists were Claude Duval and Dick Turpin.

Dressed in cloaks and three-cornered hats they became a part

of the Brighton scene. Out of this entertainment came the Jack
Sheppard concert party with a small stage and behind it a small
structure with two dressing rooms, one for men and one for
women. There was usually a cast of eight. There was an enclosure where deck chairs cost twopence and for another twopence
one could buy a photograph of the company. Once a policeman
knocked on Jack Sheppard's door at an unearthly hour to say,
'Come quickly—your stage is floating out towards France!' Later
he established a permanent site on the Madeira Lawns and a
second company was pitched by the West Pier. The artists
occasionally swopped over and dashed between 'theatres' on
bicycles.

Sheppard survived Max Miller by five years. Despite the fact
it was well known he was living alone, save for his dog, in a
two-roomed flat in Kemp Town, and he said, 'I live on three
pounds ten a week made up of my old age pension and national
assistance,' his most famous discovery Max Miller, who lived
nearby, did nothing to help rescue the old man from the poverty
of his declining years.

Max Miller joined other companies for the 1920 season, but
he returned to Jack Sheppard for the 1921 season. One member
of the cast was Winifred Butler, who was quick to spot Max
Miller's talent.

'I recollect we rehearsed at 277 Eastern Road, Brighton. Max
had a distinct personality on and off the boards. It seemed as
if he was willing himself to succeed. In those days it was possible
to get a little recording of one's voice made on the pier and
Max made one of those discs on which he said, "I am Harry
Sargent. I am Harry Sargent. I am going to become a star. I
am going to become a star!"

'Jack Sheppard was very strict. We had to dress well when we
were performing and in private life. He did not permit smoking
or swearing. I remember accompanying Mr Sheppard to the
London Palladium in 1929 to see Max Miller. He was very
proud to think he had launched a famous star.'

Ernest Bernardi recalled that Max went to see him a few days
after landing his contract with Jack Sheppard.

'He came round to me and I helped him rehearse "Give Me
The Moonlight, Give Me The Girl" and I did the arrangement

for him. Naturally I went to see the show. Max was the light comedian. His material was scripted and only later, when he took over the comedian's job, was he allowed to show individuality. Even then I did not see any amazing promise in his work. He was lively and adequate—but nothing startling. I was flabbergasted when I heard of his success a few years later. Quite frankly I never foresaw that sort of talent in him. It must have matured in the early 'twenties when he started to do a solo act.'

Max had many memories of the Jack Sheppard engagements.

'I was supposed just to sing and dance, but I used to slip in a story as well. My little gags made everybody laugh more than the comedian's stories did. That was because I was funnier, you see.

'One day Jack Sheppard came up to me and said, "What do you think of the comedian?" I was getting on pretty well then— butter on both sides of the bread—so I said, "I think he's all right in his place."

' "Where's that?" said the guv'nor.

' "Sitting in a corner saying nothing at all. Give him my job and let me be the comedian." We did change over and I got an extra two pounds fifteen a week.

'There was a chap in the company called Soapy. At one time we were giving a series of benefits for members of the company and each week we put on something special. Soapy said he once worked for an escapologist and he knew how to escape from a case that was nailed down and tied with rope.

'So Jack Sheppard announced all over the place that a marvellous bit of escaping would be performed on such-an-such a night. I don't mind telling you that the escape depended on people putting nails into holes that had already been made, and on ropes being tied that could easily be loosened and slipped over the edges of the case.

'Soapy showed us how to guide members of the audience so that they did what we wanted. On the night of the show we had a big audience. The case was brought on to the stage. Then Soapy came on and got a lot of applause. I asked for some assistants from the audience—and four sailors came up.

'Soapy got into the case, and I asked the sailors to nail on the lid and tie the ropes around it. Before I could stop them they had hammered nails into the wrong places and tied the ropes in all sorts of funny knots. I had to think quickly, so I told the audience one condition of the escape was that a screen should be placed in front of the case. So the screen was brought on.

'After a while the audience started to get restless, so I went down to the footlights and began to tell them some stories. After about fifteen minutes they began to shout things like "Where's the bloke in the case?"'

'I took a sideways look over the screen and saw Jack Sheppard trying like mad to get the nails out without making any noise. So I went on telling more gags. I don't think I've ever talked so much or so fast. It took another ten minutes for Jack to give the all clear. Then Soapy staggered out from behind the screen.

'The audience gave him a round of applause, though I think if he'd taken another five minutes to appear the whole show would have been torn to pieces.'

Max kept his first notice from a local paper, unnamed, which states :

> Mr Jack Sheppard is the doyen of concert party proprietors in Brighton, as well as one of the bright and particular stars of the Brighton and Hove Operatic Society. At his ideally pitched alfresco theatre opposite the Madeira Walk, Kemp Town, it is being given three times daily, with frequent changes in the items of the programme. As the tenor of the company, Mr Jack Sheppard is this year making a great hit with 'Jogging Along the Highway'. Mr Leonard Edwards, the refined and excellent comedian, wins high favour. Harry Sargent is the smart light comedian, and his 'Californian Girl' is a huge success.

> 'My Californian Girl
> I'll be waiting when the orange blossom grows.'

> Miss Kathleen Marsh's contralto songs are all well received, especially 'I Pass By Your Window', and she does accurate child impersonations and monologues. Miss Dora Bayham gives a fine rendering of the soprano song, 'Fifinella', and

Miss Dinkie Jeune puts great animation into 'Sporty Boys.' Miss Olive Herbert contributes merry ditties. Mr Walter Waller is the highly efficient pianist.

Max was not afraid of hard work.

'Later in the season I was asked to appear at Jack Sheppard's other concert party near the West Pier. I had to dash between each pitch by bicycle, and after a few weeks the knees of my trousers began to look very baggy. I saw myself in the mirror and roared with laughter. Suddenly it gave me the idea of wearing plus-fours. As soon as I could afford new clothes I bought a green suit with plus-fours—that was the beginning of the get-up I've become famous for wearing on the stage.

'When I used to bottle outside the enclosure, it always annoyed me that I couldn't get to the people who looked down on us from Marine Parade. I devised a ditty pole which was an enormous length of wide bamboo tubing which was fastened one end into a box and the open end was wide enough to take coins. I used to hold it up and people loved to drop pennies down into the box. We doubled the collection that way.

'Jack Sheppard liked us to hustle the crowd before the performance. That meant going round to people and saying, "Why not spend tuppence and see our show today?" Before the show started we introduced ourselves with a slogan. My one was "I'll make you laugh; I'll make you cry." '

Max Miller's first professional appearance in Brighton with Jack Sheppard's concert party made a profound impression on many people. Fifty-seven years later, over forty of them were kind enough to write with their recollections.

Mrs L Waite was born in 1901. She saw Max every Saturday.

'When we had no money to sit in the enclosure we stood at the back and we felt very mean when we moved on as the collector, or bottler, did his rounds. One day Max, then billed with his real name of Harry Sargent, appeared in plus-fours and he stood out from the rest of the company. His personality was not as strong as it became when I saw him at the Brighton Hippodrome ten years later. I remember one song he featured which we thought was very cheeky for 1919 :

"Out on the Prairie I lead a wild life
Out on the Prairie with my Prairie wife
Out on the Prairie I long to be
There I'd sit with my little Mary.
Miles and miles, away on the Prairie,
Milking the cows for the Maypole Dairy
The Prairie life for me!"

'I remember thinking to myself, "Harry Sargent is going places." I was right!'

Mr L G Russell went to see Jack Sheppard's show every evening of the 1919 season.

'Max Miller, then Harry Sargent, was the light comedian. I can still see him in my mind's eye on that side stool, looking westwards, thinking, no doubt, of the things he could do, given the chance. He sang "Give Me The Moonlight, Give Me The Girl" and "My Californian Girl".

'I used to ride on my bike between the Kemp Town show and the one opposite the Metropole and Jack Sheppard used to get his artists to rush between pitches, and Max, I recollect, used a bike too. When it rained the company played in a small hall in Madeira Drive.

'Years later, during the blitz of World War Two there was a bad raid and many were killed one afternoon in Brighton. That evening we went to see Max at the Hippodrome. The theatre was nearly empty, just a handful in the stalls and my wife and I were in the gallery. Max came on the stage, looked round the auditorium and said,

' "I'm not shouting to you lot up there—come down in the stalls!"

'We all did and we had a grand time. Happy times that I will remember always.'

Mr A E Young was interested in Max Miller's impact on audiences.

'Harry Sargent was very popular with visitors, possibly because he had a relaxed style. When he was promoted to be the comedian in 1921 he was billed as Max Miller, and he was "The Cheeky Chappie" by then, but not as blue as he became on the halls.

'Max took his turn with the other artists in going round with the collecting box through the crowds who stood beyond the enclosure. He used his ditty pole to get money from the people on the Upper Level.

'Kathleen Marsh was a striking-looking young woman who sang well in a contralto voice. She subsequently, married Max.

At the end of his first season with Jack Sheppard, Max teamed up with Kathleen Marsh to do a double act on the halls. He soon suffered the cold draught of failure and the self-confidence he gained at Brighton was soon dissipated. Kathleen Marsh was a liability and they did not rate as an entertaining duo.

Kathleen was a soubrette with a trained contralto voice. However, her repertoire was refined and did not blend well with Max's raucous voice and crude patter. They auditioned as duettists, and later as a comic adagio act, with patter and burlesque. Max bought a routine from a scriptwriter he met in an Express Dairy off Charing Cross Road.

Max : I dreamed last night that I caught a chap running away with you.
Kathleen : And what did you say to him?
Max : I asked him what he was running for.
Kathleen : They say that beauty is only skin deep.
Max : What you need is a new skin.
Kathleen : I suppose, if I died tomorrow, you'd remarry immediately.
Max : No, I'd have to take a rest first.
Kathleen : Huh! Women's minds are cleaner than men's.
Max : Yes, they keep changing them.
Kathleen : You are funny! By the way I put a shilling on a horse today.
Max : Did it fall off?
Kathleen : No man has ever made a fool out of me.
Max : Who did then?

The couple got a booking as a trial turn at the South London Palace and died a quick death. Gordon Ray, who later ran troupes of dancing girls, spoke to Max in the bar during the interval.

'Listen to me—get rid of your partner, and you may go places as a stand-up comic.'

It was three years before Max took that advice, and the moment he did his career was on the ascendancy.

The couple were waiting for a tram at the Elephant and Castle when Kathleen spotted the name Max on a hoarding. 'That's the name for you, Harry,' she said. 'Let me see, Max, Max, what goes with Max? I've got it, Miller. You must use Max Miller for stage work.'

Harry Sargent became Max Miller that day in the spring of 1920. For a time he split with Kathleen Marsh to join the touring company of Fred Roper and Bart Brady who ran a concert party called *The Rogues*.

The cast included Lily Selder, violinist; Vera Barker, comedienne; Bessie Millard, soprano; Bart Brady, comic; Alex Arnott, tenor; Max was the light comedian and he did a successful patter number with Fred Roper. He was, however, tied to a script and not allowed to exercise his individuality.

The tour was almost nationwide and took in Totnes, Tisbury, Southampton, Chard, Ilfracombe, Mumbles, Morecambe, Leamington, Douglas, Isle of Man, Chester, Glasgow, Stafford and Rhyl.

Another light comedian, Roy Denton, finished a week at the Devalance Gardens, Tenby. He had a vacant week so he went to see the follow-in show, *The Rogues*.

'It was the first time I'd seen Max Miller. He sang "There's a Little Bit of Devil in Every Little Angel", and like almost every artist in that line of business, tried to do a carbon copy of the great Fred Barnes.'

In the pub after the performance Max talked to Roy. The response to his act had only been quiet and he was worried.

'I want the truth, Roy. Exactly what do you think of me as an artist? The truth, mind.'

'Well,' said Roy Denton, 'I thought I was the worst light comedian in the business until I saw you.'

'I thought as much,' replied Max. 'The trouble is Bart Brady is the comic and he won't let me crack any gags. Comedy, that's my caper.'

A quarter of a century later Roy Denton, as a house manager, handed Max Miller seven hundred and fifty pounds for a week's work at the Norwich Hippodrome. The same sort of money came when Roy was manager at the Royal Lincoln, and Max paid an annual visit.

At the end of the season with *The Rogues*, Max stayed on a week at Rhyl. He was told one of the artists in an old-time minstrel show at the Happy Valley Amphitheatre, Llandudno, had been taken ill. Max caught the train to Llandudno, and went to see the manager, John Codman, who immediately engaged him for one month. So it was that Max plastered himself with the burnt cork of minstrelsy. He learnt to play the bones, and as Mr Bones came under the interrogation of Mr Interlocutor:

Mr Interlocutor : Are you busy these days, Mr Bones?
Mr Bones : Right up to my neck.
Mr Interlocutor : Right up to your neck, eh? What business are you in?
Mr Bones : I'm a swimming teacher. Before that I was in the hat business.
Mr Interlocutor : You surprise me, Mr Bones. What hat would you sell to a steeplejack then?
Mr Bones : A high hat.
Mr Interlocutor : A bookmaker?
Mr Bones : A Derby.
Mr Interlocutor : A blind man?
Mr Bones : A felt hat.
Mr Interlocutor : An acrobat?
Mr Bones : A spring hat.
Mr Interlocutor : A tourist?
Mr Bones : A *Cook's* hat.
Mr Interlocutor : A lazy man?
Mr Bones : A slouch hat.
Mr Interlocutor : A grave digger?
Mr Bones : A skull cap.
Mr Interlocutor : A henpecked husband?
Mr Bones : A hel—met.

Max Miller then joined the management of Ernest Binns, who

gave him a booking at the Lidget Green Pavilion, Bradford, in the spring of 1921, and a year later as a pierrot at the Shay Gardens in Halifax. Ernest Binns treasured a silver cigarette case given him by Max years later as a momento of that early engagement.

Mrs C M Haigh wrote about her memories of Max during those seasons.

'He showed distinct promise. My father, J W Bilborough, spotted his talent when he was with *The Rogues* concert party. Dad was, at the time, in partnership with Ernest Binns. They booked Max at the Arcadian Pavilion, Lidget Green, Bradford for five pounds a week. The other artists were Harry Milner, Cora Doreen, Caprice Proud, Harry Mitchell, Craig, Laurie Hardy and Rob Currie.'

In the summer of 1921 Max Miller returned to Jack Sheppard where he met up with Kathleen Marsh.

'I was very fond of her. A girl in the cast of the 1919 show, Dinkie Jeune, was a real trouble maker. When I turned her down for Kathleen she tried to get me the sack, but Jack Sheppard was clever enough to see through her little games.'

For the 1921 season he was the comedian, and his true talent was unleashed. Unfortunately when he left Jack Sheppard it took a while for managements to realise that Max could only thrive as an unscripted solo turn. He was not an actor, and to be confined to the text of a sketch was to restrict his inventive capacities.

'Well, as soon as the season was over,' recalled Max, 'up we went to London and Kathleen went to see the agent. She came back to our digs and said she didn't like his proposition. I couldn't get much more out of her than that—till a long time afterwards when she told me the truth.

'She'd kept it back because she said I was too hot-headed in those days and she was scared of what I might have done to the agent. It appears that he said he'd heard she was thinking of doing a double act with me on the halls. He told her that would do her no good. He'd put her in a show, but she'd have to forget about me.

'According to him, I was a non-runner. I had nothing to offer —no talent, no personality, nothing but a pair of long legs that

I couldn't use properly. She would have to get away from me if she wanted to get anywhere in show business—I was holding her back. Some years later I met that agent in the street. He took one look at me and scampered round the corner—so I've never had a chance to tell him what I really thought of him.'

Roy Denton said that at first glance, Max had an unfortunate appearance.

'He was over six feet tall, though not as heavy in those days. For *The Rogues* concert party he had no alternative but to squeeze in the costume the previous light comedian used. That meant his sleeves began half way up his arm and his trousers were four inches above his shoes. When he tried to do a dashing dance routine, he looked comic rather than romantic. No wonder that agent wasn't impressed!'

The well-known actor, George Graves, did see some potential in Max. He offered him the part of Count Danilo in a tour of *The Merry Widow*. But Max funked it—he was wise enough to know he was too green to go on the road in a testing acting part. 'I've always been glad I had the courage to turn down that engagement.'

Kathleen Marsh was the daughter of a Dorset blacksmith. Her brother, Alderman Ernest Marsh, was a member of Brighton Council for 43 years and a stalwart of the Labour Party. He was mayor of Brighton from 1949 to 1950.

Kathleen Marsh and Max Miller were married in 1921 and from then on Max was under the control of his wife. It is important to realise what power she gained over him and Max was completely her victim. She was of a higher social standing, educated, and a dominating personality. From the day Max was hooked he was also afraid of his wife.

Kathleen, astute woman that she was, reconciled herself to taking a back seat and promoting the career of her husband. She played an important role; she created his name, Max Miller. She spotted the description 'The Cheeky Chappie' applied to her husband in a notice, and adopted this description for his bill matter. Indeed, she was the power behind the throne and managed him throughout his career. She wrote his letters, handled his fan mail, signed his autographs, looked after his investments; in short Kathleen controlled all his affairs—apart from his very secret amorous ones!

Max, throughout his career, acknowledged the contribution made by his wife. He lovingly referred to her as 'Mum'. For an early engagement in London, at the Metropolitan Music Hall, Edgware Road, in May 1926, he took an advertisement in *The Performer* in which he stated,

'Another rose, Mamma, I've clicked again.'

In a press statement Max said,

'A great deal of my success is due to my wife. Whenever I mention it, she says, "Well, whatever I've done for you, I didn't give you your talent for making people laugh."

'In my concert party days I was pretty illiterate because I didn't have much schooling to speak of—and it was Mum who helped me along. She was my fiancée then, and she started out to improve my terrible grammar and my terrible accent, which was a mixture of cockney and Sussex dialects.

'One day she said if I taught her to dance she'd put me right on my grammar. So I agreed, and every day we had our lessons —dancing and grammar. One day an agent came round and said he'd seen the show and he was impressed by Kathleen's talent. He said he'd like to see her when the concert party finished and she went to London.'

5 The Struggling Years 1921–1929

MAX MILLER WAS determined to make it in variety. It was November 1921. Kathleen Marsh also had theatrical ambitions. Most of the pantomimes were cast, and all the agents they approached seemed uninterested. It was not until February 1922 that they accepted an offer to tour Ireland in revue.

'Digs were pretty bad in those days,' recalled Max. 'Many a time we were afraid to get in the beds for fear of being bitten to pieces by the fleas there. I decided to tell one landlady about the filthy conditions in the room she gave us.

' "My beds are the cleanest in the street!" she said. "Why I've had stars stay with me."

' "Well," I said, "they've left their stardust behind them."

'We played at Limerick during the Catholic retreat when no good Catholic must go to any sort of amusement. A priest stood at the door of the hall, taking down the names of any of his parishioners who dared to enter, so we ended up with just a handful of people.

'We all had to dress in a room beneath the stage. We had to go down some rickety stairs to get to it, and two of them were missing. This left a big gap and if you fell through it you landed in the cellar.

'I complained to a sort of general dogsbody, who called himself the manager, that the girls didn't want to dress with the boys in the same room. He seemed perplexed.

' "Why? Have you had a row?"

'In the end we rigged up a curtain to cut the place in half. The boys had to go through the girls' part to get to the stage. With the sights they saw and the conversations they heard they were men by the end of the week.

'At another town in Ireland six of us stayed in one house, paying ten bob each. The landlady was determined to teach me the Irish jig. In the end I got board and lodging, dancing lessons and a spot of company for half a quid—not a bad bargain, eh?

'The hall at Cavan was lit by candles. When the dance routines got under way the movement made by the artists blew out the candles. The stage manager had to keep a box of matches handy—the audience seemed to take it all for granted.'

Max continued with the same desultory routine when he and Kathleen joined a tour of *The Girl*, described as a 'revusical musical comedy presented by Will Gane and Cecil Morley'. After a few weeks on the road, it was patently obvious that they were not going to make it as a double act. It was surprising that they carried on for so long, but one has to remember Kathleen's dominance. Obviously she was ambitious for herself and it takes time for failure to be accepted.

Max did everything he could; he even played the straight man to Kathleen who, in one sketch, fancied herself as a dim-witted yokel with Max as an ardent artist trying to make her look like a Mona Lisa. Eccentricity is funny, but someone who is so insipid and conventional trying desperately to be odd, is merely embarrassing. Kathleen was no comedienne.

Kathleen Marsh gave up her theatrical pretentions and devoted herself to managing her husband's affairs.

Max described the difficulties he faced as an unknown comic.

'I couldn't get enough dates in variety—who could survive on one booking every ten weeks? The only thing I was offered was touring revue which I hated, but it gave me long engagements at a regular salary. I had to act in sketches, but I always made sure I was given a solo spot. I was able to polish my act, and then, between revues, I usually managed to fix a few bookings doing my front-cloth turn.

'I remember being in a show called *There You Are Then*, a so-called "Sixty Mile An Hour Jazz Revue" and it did pretty well at the small theatres. I was given some tuition in dancing and singing and during that run I developed a burlesque routine, taking the piss out of toffee-nosed vocalists who thought they were the greatest thing to walk the boards. In those days British artists had started to ape the Americans, and that's still going on today. The only way to become a star is to develop your own style, which owes nothing to anybody else.

'I remember seeing Layton and Johnstone, two coloured blokes with piano accompaniment. The greatest turn of its kind ever. When Turner Layton went solo, he was streets ahead of "Hutch", another coloured singer. I never tried to ape anybody; but Turner Layton taught me to try to sing in a lilting, melodious way.

'It gave me a pain to see a comic work a gag to death. They'd build an act round a dozen gags. That's not value for money. I'd pack 'em in quick and they hadn't time to think too long over the duds, see?

'I found that if I told a story a certain way the audience began to laugh before I got to the end. They thought they knew the answer, see? They were laughing at their own jokes. A parson once complained to me that I was too vulgar for his daughter. I said, "Well, she must know a thing or two then, mustn't she?"

'Why does everybody begin to laugh when I say, "There was a young lady from Tooting..." They expected something terrible. The last time they saw me I'd said, "There was a young lady from Tottenham, her manners she'd quite forgotten 'em". A bit more, see? When they came the second time, they thought, blimey, he's coming out with a shocker! What's in your mind when I say, "I heard the front door bell ring. I jumped out of the bath, put on my wife's kimono, and opened the door, and the postman kissed me"? That I'm really a great big pouf, or he'd mistaken me for the wife. Take your choice.

'There are two sorts of laugh: *at* and *with*. I hoped the public would do both when I was on the stage. It was easy for me to be cheeky and audiences liked it that way. Another thing, some comics stood ten feet back from the floats, like ruddy statues, with a spot straight on 'em. I wanted to get near the customers just like the bloke in the bar who says, "Heard this one?" He takes the listeners into his confidence. I took a whole theatreful of people into my confidence.

'Of course I had doubts. I'd go to a filthy old theatre, come Monday, for the band call. The paint was peeling off the walls, smelly places they were, and the boys in the pit, half of 'em didn't know a hatchet from a crotchet. The stage manager would say, "Miller, second spot, ten minutes." I felt like answering, You bloody fool. If I can keep 'em interested for twenty minutes it ain't goin' to cost you. And next week they'll come back because they thought I was good and you might have another treat in store. Instead, they went to the flicks in the flea pit next door.

'Again, on the way back to the digs, standing at that bus stop with rain pissin' down your bleedin' neck . . . 'cause I got worried. Not because I was a dud, but because variety theatres were closing down, and soon there'd be nowhere for me to do my act. As a matter of fact those fears were justified—it took thirty years to kill off the music hall, that's all.

'I tried out my singing again in a show called *Crisps*. Then I was in *Capital Levy*, a comedy written to exploit the character comedian Ernie Lotinga who played a crazy bailiff who got on to a guy who was late in paying his rent.'

In 1925 Max joined Clara Coverdale's successful sporting revue, *Ten To One On*, in which the fertile and unusual comedian Jimmy James was the star, showing off his versatility in a number of sketches. Max Miller was unhappily cast as a light comedian, and there were no opportunities for him to show off his talent for comedy.

'I reckon about one in every two hundred pros make it. I was determined not to be a failure. I knew I'd got talent, but I needed the opportunities. I used to study Jimmy James, a marvellous artist and his little sketches showed the audience a character who was believable, but unlike anybody they'd ever seen in real life. Jimmy never got the breaks he deserved.

'I didn't mind working the tat halls, it gave me the experience I needed. By trial and error I got an act together and I learnt how to put it across. I became relaxed and I improved my timing. I'd buy gags and I dreamt up the rest myself. I knew the sort of story that would make people laugh. Few writers understood my requirements.

'The public told me I was doing all right—they laughed at

me, and that's what sold me to managers. They say I'm "stingy Miller". My policy has been to give, but only to deserving cases. Right back in the 'twenties I made it my way. I didn't buy favours. That policy turned out right for me too. Agents thought, he must be doing well if he doesn't bother to buy me a drink. They gave me bookings for insulting 'em.

'I used to look at other pros and I'd pick up a few hints from 'em—never copied 'em, mind. Like George Robey—he was still good; he knew about timing a line. Then, in 1930 I was on the bill with him at the Victoria Palace, and, blimey, he'd just gone over the top—you know what I mean, he'd lost that bit of magic, and after that it was down, down till he ended up as a pathetic old man, trading on sympathy. Took the next twenty years to hit rock bottom; he should have packed it in by 1940.

'Come 1925 I'd think to myself the public's got to say, "Miller —ah, he's a bloke worth buying a ticket to see." How did I set about it? By looking different and being unique—the one and the only, see?'

Max Miller developed his front-cloth act in cine-variety. The idea of acts in cinemas began before the First World War. It was a make-weight device, tolerated by audiences more interested in watching films. Comedians, vocalists and speciality turns often had an uphill battle, especially when abuse was thrown at them. Young people paid their pennies to canoodle in the privacy of darkness. Max was once on the bill with a veteran music-hall artist, Victoria Monks.

'Victoria Monks was once a big star, but she was down in her luck when she got this date in a flea pit in South London. Her dress was all tattered and even when she sang "Won't You Come Home, Bill Bailey?" the rowdies gave her the bird good and proper. I didn't do much better. I used to keep my best stuff for variety and I used to try out some cheap gags to see if they'd get across. You know the sort of thing :

' "I was talking to this girl and I told her what nice hands she'd got—and nice nails too. I said, 'Do you file them?' and she said, 'No, I just throw them away.'

' "I had a tough childhood, lady. I wasn't even born. I was laid. On a doorstep. Isn't the conductor fat? Listen—listen, he can't even get into a phone box unless he pushes button B and

63

then his penny keeps falling out . . . now make something of that, filthy lot."

' "When I was in the army the Colonel said, 'Send reinforcements. I am going to advance.' I got it all wrong. I thought he said, 'Send three and fourpence, I'm going to a dance.'

> ' "There was a young woman from Devizes
> She had tits of different sizes;
> One was so small
> It was no use at all;
> The other was so big, it won prizes." '

Soon the cinema organ was the sole survivor of the vogue for cine-variety. Max worked up his burlesque of American-style vocalists. This act held him in good stead for seven years. His wardrobe was loud. In 1925 he wore a hideous green plus-fours-style suit with a canary-yellow trilby upturned to show off his twinkling blue eyes. The floral suit came in the following years.

The well-known musical director Hugh James remembered Max in those days.

'I think it was early in 1926. I was conductor at the Putney Hippodrome where cine-variety was the attraction. Max received three pounds for a split week of three days. His act didn't set the world on fire. We in the pit orchestra regarded him as just another comedian. He also worked the Shakespeare, Clapham, Woolwich and the Mile End Empire. Max would invite me into his dressing room and ask my opinion about his compositions which he strummed out on a guitar. I'd give him some advice on presentation.'

Mr T W Hendrick was in the audience at the Putney Hippodrome for the half week of cine-variety recalled by Hugh James.

'It was the first time I'd seen Max Miller. He wore this baggy green plus-fours suit. He delivered some quickfire patter. Then, with sham emotion, he burlesqued the number "Broken Hearted", which brought the house down. He pretended to complain to the manager that the audience wouldn't take him seriously, and he refused to continue until we all persuaded him to start again with :

The Struggling Years 1921-1929

"There she goes—my best girl.
There she goes—my best pal.
And here am I—broken hearted." '

The operatic tenor George L Colebrooke remembered Max
when he was booked to sing in a cinema in Teddington in 1926.

'I shared the bill with another artist. I walked into my dressing
room on the Friday night to find my agent, who introduced me
to a young man with him, tall and good looking. The agent said
he wanted to get "his nose into variety". The agent asked me
to cut a few minutes out of my act, and my fellow artist likewise,
so he could put Max on to see what he could do in front of an
audience. We agreed to his request.

'Max dressed in a bowler hat and a brightly coloured chintz
overcoat over ordinary clothes. He opened with a humorous
song, told some gags and closed with a quick moving ditty. As
an encore he did an acrobatic dance which included some cart-
wheels. He went over well but the agent was not enthusiastic
about his act. A couple of years later I spotted an advert in the
professional press : "Don't whistle. I'm not looking back—Max
Miller."

'In 1938 I saw him at the London Palladium. His act used
more blue material. He had cut out the acrobatic dancing. A
friend told me he'd developed bunions.'

Many correspondents told me Max Miller exercised remarkable command over an audience by 1926. Mr F H Marsden
wrote :

'Some Friday nights cinemas needed a boost, and at the Grand
Kinema, in the Edgware Road, opposite Harrow Road, I saw
Max Miller as one of six turns in *Friday Night is Variety Night*.

'Max was so outstanding he made a lasting impression on me.
He wore an outrageous suit, a white hat and correspondent's
shoes. He cracked some saucy gags, sang a couple of songs, and
did a neat soft shoe dance to the music of Jack Leon's band.
He did a routine I saw him repeat in variety at the Metropolitan Music Hall in Edgware Road a little later—of putting
up his hands to ward off imaginary missiles he expected to receive
from the audience. He didn't get anything thrown at him when
I was out front. He had the ability of keeping that house laughing

non-stop all through his act. Even then, his timing and the power of his personality made him unique. I have seen every top liner since, but nobody had Max's genius.'

The Performer noted Max's date at the Metropolitan for the week 17th May 1926. 'Max Miller executes a neat dance and makes a sure success with a string of laughable patter.' Max inserted this notice in that paper : 'Another Rose, Mamma, I've clicked again.'

Two weeks later, at the London, Shoreditch, *The Encore* wrote :

'A comedian of the new school, Max Miller, created a great impression with a budget of quaintly humorous and topical gags and excellent songs. His methods are original and his style is unique.'

Max was billed as 'The new comedian—a certain cure for sadness'. He and Kathleen found digs at 257 Kennington Road, in South London, which they used whenever Max got a London date or was unemployed. In August 1926 he advertised in *The Stage* :

> Watch my smoke !
> The inexhaustible comedian
> Last week a riot at Birkenhead.
> This week raising the roof at Poole.

In *The Encore* he advised readers to 'Watch this kid Max Miller !' His advice was accepted and he got a booking at the Holborn Empire, one of London's leading variety houses, and Max's second home throughout the 1930s. He was on a bill including the twenty-stone maestro of the xylophone, Teddy Brown, the Café de Paris Band, and the Irish ballad singer, Talbot O'Farrell. *The Stage* warned him about using 'stale jokes' but *The Encore* had nothing but praise.

'Max Miller nearly caused a riot with his particular brand of humour and in spite of trying to quieten the audience, they wanted more. This boy will go far. He has a personality and a way of getting his gags over which distinctly appeals. It's not what he says, though there's not an unfunny remark in his repertoire, but how he says it.'

Max was so pleased with the reception given by *The Encore* he inserted an advertisement saying : 'Max Miller. The inexhaustible comedian. We said we would !'

Max took an agent to represent him called George Sax. He was advised to reject an offer of a tour in a revue for a well-known company, Reeves and Lamport, and to turn down another engagement with the old-timer Ada Reeve. A young impresario, Tom Arnold, who had spotted Max at the Holborn Empire, offered him the star part in a revue by Ronald Jeans called *Piccadilly*. He accepted and the show opened in Birmingham in November 1926. Max's co-star was another young and relatively unknown artist, 21-year-old Florence Desmond. They both justified Arnold's confidence.

Piccadilly had lavish settings and was well choreographed. Max scored in a coster scene, 'Southend', and in a sketch with Florence Desmond, 'Catching the Male'. As was to be expected Max had difficulty in fitting into a scripted show, as Florence Desmond recalled.

'Max was a brilliant comedian. He knew exactly how to put over a cheeky gag and he had a way with a song too. However, I cannot say he was a nice man. As an artist he was selfish. It was almost impossible to play a scene with him. He was out to exploit the comedy for himself, and being a front-cloth comedian, he used the technique of playing outwards instead of to me.'

Tom Arnold took Max to task saying that his selfishness was spoiling the balance of the show and if he did not conform he could do without him. As a result Max left the tour after ten weeks. He resumed his career in variety at the Palace, Oldham, on 31st January 1927 where the local critic, grammar apart, made a surprising observation.

'Max Miller is one of the most laughable comedians to have visited Oldham for some time. His humour lacks the slightest suggestiveness and is of a type which rests in a far higher plane than that used by many who have world wide popularity.'

With only one date in his book, Max took fright, and accepted an offer to take over in a revue already on tour called *The Show*. Max remembered the manager who presented the piece, the legendary Fred Karno.

'Karno had a big reputation, but by the time I worked for

him he was on the skids. He'd lost a fortune at that fun palace of his, Karsino, on Tagg's Island, near Hampton Court.

'I didn't like his manner. He treated me as if he was hiring me to be his gardener, not to star in a show for him. Rough he was too, blimey, I spoke better grammar than he did.

' "You might do I suppose," said Karno.

'I chipped in dead quick, I can tell you. "Listen, Talbot O'Farrell told me you'd seen me work in *Piccadilly* and you thought I'd be great for your revue."

' "What I did say, Miller, was that I could use you. Don't you start telling me how good you were in *Piccadilly* either. Remember, it's today what counts in this business, not what you did last week."

' "I got some bloody fine notices."

' "If you're thinking of collecting notices to dazzle people with, forget that too. There's only one thing an old review is good for, Miller—and that's to wipe your arse with. Now, down to brass tacks, what's your money?"

' "Twenty quid a week."

' "You are a comedian—but not a very funny one. You can halve that."

' "You can, mate, but I'm not going to."

' "Bit of an auctioneer, eh, Miller?"

' "You said it, Karno. Eighteen quid."

' "I've said it, twelve."

' "All right—but if you're not worth it . . ." snapped Karno.

' "Split the difference—fifteen."

'Things were a bit dicey at Glasgow. There was a mix-up with my band parts and the orchestra had to busk one of my numbers —a right balls-up it was—and just my luck, the guv'nor, Karno, was out front, see. Sure as God made little apples, he comes round in the interval. He opened the door of my dressing room and he just stared at me. At last he spoke.

' "And to think I paid Charlie Chaplin three fucking pounds a week."

'With that he walked out of the room.

'The next time Karno came round everything went over big but he didn't want to let on he was pleased.

' "Didn't I get some great laughs, Mr Karno?"

' "Yes, you weren't too bad—but the rest of the show—it's falling apart. I want my artists to give everything they've got; to sweat blood for me. A few double acts, that's what's needed to liven it all up a bit."

' "But I'm a solo turn. I work alone."

' "I don't mean that sort of double act, you twerp. I mean fuck a few of the chorus girls, Miller. That'll make 'em happy and that's good for the production. It'll show, it'll show."

Max Miller came out of *The Show* at Kingston in May 1927 where it was said of him, 'He has a style that compels laughter. The audience eats up his comedy like hot cakes.'

The Millers took a new home at 17 Camelford Street, Brighton, and a week after closing for Karno, Max opened a tour of a revue called *XYZ* at Ramsgate. He tried his hand in a cod ballet, was successful in sketches, although when he reached Southport on 27th June the local critic noted; 'He is best with the stage to himself.' This view was supported by another artist in the company, Nellie Sheffield.

'I used to be known as a gagster. I'd slip in something topical for a laugh. Did I have a taste of my own medicine with Max Miller! We did one routine where I played his doting mother. I've always been pretty shrewd when it comes to holding my own, but I couldn't keep track of Max Miller.

'He'd upstage me, and, behind my back, he'd do a whole routine when I was trying to get a line across. Max would think of a gag, he'd rehearse it to himself, and then he'd slip it in without warning. Wham! If it went over well he'd work in three or four more; instead of a duologue, he'd end up doing a patter act and I'd have to stand there with an egg on my face.

'I went to the stage manager and I said I couldn't continue unless Max behaved himself. A rehearsal was called and Max was most annoyed and he said,

' "Listen, I'm the star. Who are you to lay down conditions? If I get laughs it's good for the show and for business. Blimey, the script needs a rewrite anyway. If a joke hits me I want to try it."

' "Yes, but there are limits, Max," I said. "This is a book show, and everybody's got to act as written."

' "Well, if that's it, I don't like it," replied Max. "If we can't work together, let's call it quits."

' "That's all right by me," I said. "And I'm the one who'll have to go, I suppose. If you carry on like this, Max, you'll never make an actor."

' "I don't want to be an actor. I'm a comic. I work better alone."

'How right he was!'

When *XYZ* reached Nottingham in November, in a scene in which Max interrupted the ramblings of an octogenarian, he was described as 'a cornucopia of mirth; it's a revelation in comedy'.

Max left *XYZ* in December to take up a string of dates offered by the impresario Charles Gulliver, including two visits to the Holborn Empire, in January and April 1928. The second visit saw Max on a strong bill, with the Australian entertainer, Albert Whelan, Fred Duprez, 'The American Arch Joker,' Dorothy Ward the vocalist and principal boy of pantomime, and the comic Ernie Mayne, who appeared as a schoolmaster, and who sang about 'The Blushing Bride That Wasn't To Be.'

Dorothy Ward said of Max,

'He was a fine artist. As a man I can't say he was pleasant to know. He promised to bring me a delicious fresh duck from Brighton on the final Saturday of the engagement. He brought it in, wrapped up in a box. I paid for it. Only when I reached home, did I discover it was rotten and had to be thrown away immediately.'

Max took the advice of *The Stage* by investing in new gags. *The Encore* applauded his fresh patter: 'Witty, very piquant, and satirical. He shows pronounced powers of showmanship.'

Max continued in variety until the end of July when he went into rehearsals for an elaborate revue called *Tipperary Tim* in which he played the title role. It opened at the Alhambra, Bradford, in August to an enthusiastic press. Presented by the northern impresario, Francis Laidler, no expense was spared in the production. The story was of an Irish woman who inherited a fortune and went to London with her son, Tim, to invest the money. Max made much of the scenes in which he sowed his wild oats and as *The Encore* noted:

70

'He has a mysterious natural gift of putting himself on good terms with the audience the moment he steps on the stage.'

The Stage said, 'He sang, danced, joked and smiled his way into favour and took numerous curtains.'

Max worked his burlesque of 'Broken Hearted' into the show which toured with great success until March 1929. He had split with George Sax before *Tipperary Tim* and it was when he returned to variety at the Hippodrome, Brighton, in March 1929, that he became represented by Julius Darewski, who was to remain his agent until his death.

Max was reluctant to go into any more revues. A number of big theatres in the provinces had abandoned twice-nightly revues in favour of once nightly plays and musicals. The lesser revues played second-rate dates to bad business, owing to their lack of inspiration and the popularity of cinema going.

Max's theory was proved right when he reappeared at the Holborn Empire in March 1929 when *The Encore* said, 'He is a born comedian whose style is so natural, the house rose at him.'

In April Max played a split week of three nights at the Canterbury and three nights at East Ham. The juggler Billy Gray was on the bill.

'I shall never forget seeing Max work for the first time at the Canterbury. He wore a black and white plus-fours suit, with black linoleum on his lapels, and sets of false bananas on each shoulder. He made his entrance riding on an ostrich. This consisted of a man in an ostrich skin. Max gave him ten bob for the job out of his salary of four pounds for the split week of three nights.

'Many years later I worked with Max at Coventry when he came up to me and showed me a cheque for one week's engagement, of £1,025. He said, "A bit better than when I worked three nights at the Canterbury for four quid, eh, Bill?"

'Max was a great artist in 1929—he just needed that bit of polish and better material, and as you know, within a short space of time he was Britain's biggest name in variety.'

In May 1929 George Black engaged Miller for the London Palladium and *The Encore* noted, 'He collared the audience the moment he faced them and he kept them busy laughing from the start to the finish of his act.'

The Palladium had been taken over by the two million pound company, The General Theatre Corporation, in 1928. Within a year of his appointment to the board, the showman George Black assumed responsibility for the Palladium, and he controlled the destiny of this theatre until his death in 1945. He màde people know he was the boss. He said to Val Parnell, the booking manager, whom he considered too outspoken as a minion :

'If you want to stay in that seat, Parnell, it'll be a question of playing Caesar's Wife and that means you must be above reproach.'

George Black did more to keep variety alive than anybody else. The public came under the spell of lavish filmed musicals made in Hollywood. Black was influenced too, and it showed in the way he staged his bills. His presentations were slick, swift and well dressed. Honest vulgarity didn't bother him. In criticising a comic's routine he once said, 'It's dull, lose your pants.' To Max Miller, with whom he negotiated his Palladium booking of 1929, 'I'll give you twelve pounds a week, and another fiver if you spend it on new material.'

Black ruthlessly pruned the scripts. Words like 'that reminds me of the story . . .' before the gag was cracked were out. Black placed a turn in a full set. Then, just preceding the *pièce de resistance*, the artist would move towards the floats and the tabs would close behind him. Then, no sooner than he was off, the new introductory music would begin, the tabs would open, and the next act was on its way. This sort of staging is commonplace in 1977. It was revolutionary in 1929.

George Black described Max Miller's apprenticeship :

'I did not discover Max Miller. No one did. He was playing the halls for years, long before his name got into big letters. He worked his way up in the profession.

'When I first came to London and took over variety in a big way, Max Miller was hanging around the background waiting for his break. I knew it was coming. In those days Max used to drive an old, bull-nosed Morris Cowley—a most dilapidated outfit. He was a cheeky chappie in real life.

'Max would come wafting into my office two or three times a week, trying to persuade me to give him bookings. He would put it over on me just as he does his audiences. Although he made me a trifle more generous than I might have been, I knew he was going to be worth it one day.

'Max was a small-time comic then, drawing seventeen pounds a week. He soon got big money because he was a worker who put his heart and soul into making himself funny. There's no nonsense about Max. When his job is done he dashes off to his wife and home in Brighton.'

The Crazy Gang became a regular feature at the Palladium. Early on during their partnership onstage fooling was getting out of control and a backstage dispute threatened the future of the show. George Black called a rehearsal at ten o'clock one morning. He gave each artist a terrific dressing-down and he ended up with this observation :

'You're all bloody lucky to be here. As acts outside the Crazy Gang, you'd be hard pushed to make a living. Take Max Miller —he's got more talent in his little finger than any of you have got in your whole body—remember that !'

It was in 1957 that Max's agent, Julius Darewski, spoke about his client.

'I've been his agent for thirty years and I like to think I've been his friend as well. I saw Max work when he was quite small time, around 1927. I remember thinking to myself, "This boy's got star quality." He needed the chance to get somewhere.

'He was wearing his famous plus-fours even then. It was a really striking get-up and part of his professional hallmark. You can imagine my surprise when I went along to the Palladium to see him work there, and found he was wearing an ordinary suit.

'It seemed that George Black had said, "Why do you wear those idiotic clothes? Get into a lounge suit." Well, Max had to do what he was told. Of course, he went on as the second act following the Palladium girls—and he was a flop. That was when I took Max under my wing. I told him it was all wrong for him to work in an ordinary suit and that he must go back to the plus-fours outfit. He did, and he was a terrific success. He paralysed 'em. His money went up and from that time onwards, Max Miller never looked back.'

Another George Black innovation was to have not one, but three top of the bill turns. For example when Max played the

Palace, Blackpool, in June 1929 he shared top spot with Will Hay and Nat Mills and Bobbie, a forthright man and his soppy woman companion, a classic in vaudeville acts. From there Max went into a 'Number One Summer Season Spectacular,' *The Show of Shows* at the Winter Gardens, Blackpool, for Julian Wylie.

Max was no sooner back in London than he was at the Holborn Empire, where *The Encore* offered some advice : 'His talents are too rare to be swallowed up in a production. He should stay in London for six months.'

It was during a week at the Palladium in October that Max disregarded that sound opinion. He was offered three times his Palladium salary to tour in a revue *Fools in Paradise*. It consisted of twelve sketches and Max shared the comedy with a well-known duo, the O'Gorman Brothers. The diminutive comic Jack Marks was partnered by Ivy Luck, and a highlight of the show had Marks as a park keeper who had lost his keys, trapped in the park with the attractive Miss Luck. The soubrette was Doris Hare, who showed great promise as a dancer and in her solo spot she did impersonations, with her sister, Winnie Braemar, at the piano. Doris Hare remembered Max with affection.

'He was young and good looking, and he was a long way towards perfecting his act. It was obvious he was going to be a big star. The O'Gormans were a routine double act, and they were frightfully jealous of Max who was way out in front when it came to talent.

'I remember going round Woolworths with the O'Gormans who made several purchases, which they loaded on tiny Jackie Marks; of course, the inevitable happened with much breaking of cheap china and glass."

Winnie Braemar had an unusual memory of Max.

'We were on a railway station and Max began to unbutton the top buttons of his flies. No salacious intentions—it was, we found out, the first step towards loosening the corset he always wore, which, incidentally, gave him much discomfort. It was too tight for him.'

The actor, writer and entrepreneur Jack Marks was always on the lookout for talent.

'I first spotted Max Miller in small revues touring in the

north country. When he was playing parts he was terrible. Then I saw him as second turn at the London Palladium and as a stand-up comic—terrific.

'Max was always looking for ways of making a quick few pennies. He'd invite Val Parnell down to Brighton and then charge him ten shillings a lesson to teach him to play golf.

'I was going into *Fools in Paradise* and I got my agent, Harry Norris, to put up Max for the show. As I was dealing with contracts I asked Max what he wanted.

' "Fifty pounds a week."

'I decided to offer him forty—knowing the top figure was forty-five.'

' "No, I want to stick out for fifty," said Max.

' "My top figure is forty-five. Take it or leave it," I said. "You're not worth more."

' "Listen," said Max. "Make it fifty pounds and I'll spend five pounds a week on you. Failing that I'll give you back a fiver."

' "Yes, but what's the point of that, Maxie?"

' "Well," answered Max, "If I can say I'm on fifty a week— it's my first step towards saying 'I want a hundred a week.' Forty-five—that doesn't sound so good, see?"

'I told Norris about the conversation, but said to him on no account should he mention to anyone about Max's salary.

'Well, Harry Norris was in the bar at the Palladium one night and after he had a few drinks, he told George Black, who was paying Max seventeen pounds a week at the Palladium as second turn. "Apart from the fact you are paying him double what you should, everybody knows Max Miller is hopeless at speaking lines —he can't act for toffee."

' "Yes, but we're getting him to do his act as well."

' "You're still crazy," said Black.

'Not so long after that George Black was paying Max six hundred pounds a week.

'The O'Gorman Brothers were notoriously difficult to work with; they had co-star billing with Max Miller in *Fools in Paradise* and it was decided that they had the number one dressing room on alternate weeks—Max occupying it on the week they humbled themselves to occupy number two.

'We opened at Birmingham on the eleventh of November 1929, and the show was not a success. Max was hopeless in the sketches. I had to do a lot of rewrites and I cut his parts down. In order to justify his salary I gave him a longer spot with his own act. He was a riot.

'The next date was the Empire, Swansea. The O'Gorman Brothers went against their agreement. Joe O'Gorman said, "Miller has been cut down in the sketches. He doesn't justify co-star billing and from now on we're taking the number one dressing room *every* week."

'Max Miller stood out for his rights. In the end I telephoned Harry Norris in London. He came down and Miller had his way but only after he had threatened to leave that afternoon. Norris was very rude to him and told him that if he did that word would get around and he'd be blacklisted.

'That night Max was a sensation with his act; thereafter he got all the best notices and eventually he left the show when we had some bad weeks and couldn't pay the full salaries.

'The original presenter of *Fools in Paradise* had raised the capital by defrauding his former employer, Tom Walls. He ended up in prison. I was advised to serve notice on him in the prison. Then at the Kingston Empire I arrived with bailiffs and took the show over, running it with the O'Gormans. They eventually froze me out.

'Money meant a lot to Max. He liked to brag to people about the enormous fees he received. I remember on the tour he'd wear his best suits at the train calls, and he hoped that other pros and managers would spot him at Crewe. To make sure he'd flash a diamond ring in their faces. A few years previously he was so shabby even the top of his shoes were departing from the soles.

'If you want an apt description of Max Miller I'd say he was a lovable rogue.'

John A Boardman wrote to tell me he saw Max in *Fools in Paradise* at Southampton.

'I met him in the bar and I told him he did not have enough to do in the sketches. He merely nodded. When he did his act he had a unique way of pointing his gags. I remember one to this day.

"I was giving this girl a lift down the Brighton Road when

76

my car broke down. I said, My car's broken down. She answered, Don't be a fool, Maxie, this is a main road." '

At the Metropolitan in *Fools in Paradise*, his singing of 'When You are Gone' with the backing of the Coney Islanders singing group, was a hit and his parody of the sentimental number, 'Broken Hearted', had the house in stitches. Bookers were in front and Max ended 1929 with a string of engagements for the New Year.

6   Success 1930–1932

THE YEAR 1930 was the beginning of prosperity for Max Miller. Under the careful guidance of his agent Julius Darewski he got top of the bill spots in suburban and provincial houses. Furthermore, with well-publicised successes at the Holborn Empire and the London Palladium, he became the talk of the profession.

Mr H Frampton, who was born in 1883, wrote to me about his visit to the Holborn Empire in 1930.

'I took my niece to see Max Miller, the embodiment of a "Cheeky Chappie". He strolled on the stage in his whimsical way, and gazed at the audience in a pleasantly defiant manner. Full of assurance, he seemed to address my niece and the entire audience at the same time when he said, "Nice figure I've got, ain't I, ducks?"

'Well, my niece, who was convinced Max had directed this observation at her, fell about laughing. When Max ogled his lovely blue eyes at her, that was altogether too much for the girl, and she went into hysterics. By that time the entire audience was screaming with laughter. All this, and Max had only uttered one line!

' "Now, this is no laughing matter, miss," said Max, wagging a critical eye at my niece.

'That didn't stop her, so Max said, "Now, girl, if you're going to spoil the show by laughing at me, I may have to ask you to leave." Everybody was screaming by that time and Max said, "Crikey, I can't ask you all to leave, can I?" '

Max had the capacity of quelling a hostile element in an audience. Sidney G Ramell was serving in the Royal Navy when he saw Max at the King's Theatre, Southsea.

'I think the old adage, "It takes a clever man to be a fool" could well be applied to the late Max Miller. Add to this his charm and one could understand his appeal. He had only to walk on the stage in that flowered suit and everybody was enraptured. What a charmer he was!

'He waited for the applause to die down and almost as an aside he said, "How do you like it, girls? Lovely, isn't it? A great, big—pint of beer."

'The stage box was occupied by a lieutenant-commander in full naval uniform, who was the worse for drink. He was accompanied by a flashy female. The officer started cracking his own jokes. Max went over to him, and as he did so he called out to the man operating the limes, "Here, put a spot on this geezer." Max addressed the officer: "Listen, if you want to do my act, you come on the stage and I'll go up there with the blonde. If you don't fancy that, keep quiet."

'In a flash the house took up Max's challenge and started booing, loud and long, and the two occupants of the box withdrew almost behind the curtains in their embarrassment. Max said, "What an advert for the Navy! I was in the Army myself." He then continued with his act.'

The actor and comedian Fred MacNaughton was an admirer of Max.

'Max Miller was the greatest front-cloth comic I have ever seen—better than George Robey. He had Robey's talent and sex appeal. Max was so powerful that he could hold the attention of a vast audience with the slenderest material. I first met him in the late 'twenties when he took over in a revue called *The Lido Follies* at the New Cross Empire.

'I saw Max a little later at the Stratford Empire as a solo turn. He had mastered that great facility of his for confiding in his audience. You'd marvel at the sheer audacity of the man when he said, "Pretty, aren't I, lady? No, don't laugh. All right, one fool at a time, please."

'Max Miller created his own type. He was inimitable.'

When Max played in cine-variety at the Mile End Empire he did three shows a day. After a few gags he said, 'This lark's killing me. I think I'll have a little sleep.' He lay on the stage, closed his eyes, and a recording of his act was played over a loudspeaker.

1930 was a busy year. At the Finsbury Park Empire a scribe observed, 'The "Cheeky Fellow" had them shrieking at him.' He played in cinemas at Dover, New Cross and Stratford East, and leading variety houses like the Hippodromes at Bristol, Portsmouth and Brighton, the Victoria Palace, the Penge Empire, the Shepherd's Bush Empire where he was an all-time favourite, the Palace, Walthamstow, the Hackney Empire and back to the Holborn Empire, where he frequently appeared throughout the 1930s. Of his performance in 1930 the well-known critic, M Willson Disher, wrote :

'There is a refreshing originality and inimitably comic character about Max Miller's particular brand of humour that reduces audiences to a state of helpless hilarity. Inexhaustible is certainly the adjective to apply to his powerful and ringing voice, his resources of wit, his collection of gags and his command of repartee. They simply shrieked at Max Miller here, as they do everywhere else, and his applause was bigger than that accorded many star artists. Max Miller is, in one bound, a star of the first water.'

Max Miller had arrived.

Max went on to the Hippodromes at Leeds and Newcastle before returning to the London Palladium where Disher observed :

'Max Miller's new brand of humour amuses us more every time we have the opportunity of listening to it.'

George Robey was sixty-one and past his prime. Unwittingly, Robey had paved the way for Max. At one time there was an outcry against Robey's material which he described as 'honest vulgarity'. His tilt against propriety was one aspect of a revolt against outmoded conventions and brought about a new freedom for comedians to make fun of hitherto private aspects of human behaviour.

Audiences who saw Max in West End theatres in 1930 were able to compare him with the best of the old school. When Max played the London Coliseum, a critic wrote :

'He excels himself with confidential humour which we must ever prize because, without it, music hall would surely die.'

On the same programme was the superb female impersonator, G S Melvin, who, on being asked how he managed to keep on top so long, replied, 'I am not content to rest on my laurels. I am constantly inventing new characters, based in large measure on people who strike me as funny or unusual. The public has the right to expect something new from a variety artist.'

At the London Palladium a month later, Max was on the bill with Harry Lauder, the bandy-legged Scot who could sing a ballad in an unrivalled way. Lauder was still popular though, in common with other veteran artists, he churned out the same stale material year after year, relying on the indulgence of the sentimental British public.

With such a personality Lauder did not need to assume other characters. Similarly Max Miller was a personality comedian. He was too arrogant to be anybody else but the Cheeky Chappie. He could not shed his skin. He found the right formula which was safe and strong and he could not venture from it. By the 1950s Max was regurgitating exactly the same act he had given at the Holborn Empire twenty-five years earlier. However, his magnetism overrode this weakness.

In 1930 Max did two seasons of cabaret at the Café de Paris. He was an instant success because he was news. A few years later he reappeared there and it was an uphill struggle for him. The Café had become the haunt of Douglas Byng's admirers, and this great artist, the ultimate in sophistication, had to replace Max before the end of his season. Max needed a big theatre for his effects—cabaret, films, radio and television offered him opportunities but in every instance the work was alien to him.

Back at the Holborn Empire, enthusiastic praise was showered on Max who made his entrance to cries of 'Welcome back!'

'Familiar chirpiness won him all hearts. There is a widespread eagerness to hear him. He is much talked about which shows that in his choice of clothes, jests and songs he shows a clear sense of style.'

Max returned to a star-studded bill at the London Palladium. It included Robb Wilton's studies in bundling officialdom and Sam Mayo, 'The Immobile Comedian', who taught Max a few tricks in confiding his songs and patter to an audience. Finally, Sophie Tucker's ringing voice and showwomanship gave British audiences a taste of top American vaudeville. Max was a riot. 'His effervescent spirit makes us optimistic about life. Everybody agrees his success is well deserved. It is a pleasure to watch his progress.'

1930 had been a testing year for the variety theatre. It attempted, not very successfully, to compete with the immense popularity of talking pictures. Variety stars were foolish enough to outprice themselves. Nobody wanted them at their inflated salaries. The managers didn't; the rank and file turns, who existed on small fees in order that the top of the bill could receive hundreds, never welcomed the trend, and the public's support wavered.

Audiences realised that a big name at the top of the bill meant cheap acts on the rest of the programme. This trend climaxed in December 1930 with the booking of Maurice Chevalier for a personal appearance at the Dominion Cinema in London. Box office returns did not justify his inflated salary of £4,000 a week. When the fans found no trouble in getting in they were even more disappointed to sit through an indifferent supporting bill. Once bitten twice shy. Boredom is too painful to be forgotten.

In February 1931 Max did cabaret at the Trocadero and the success he achieved there was repeated at Frascati's in March. He returned to the London Coliseum, where the proprietor, Sir Oswald Stoll, was well known for his use of the blue pencil. On the nights when his puritanical employer was out of London, Max slipped in a few risqué jokes—he explained his action to the nervous stage manager by saying, 'I'll lose my reputation otherwise, mate.'

After a number of provincial dates, Max received the accolade of stardom when he was invited to appear in his first Royal Variety Show at the London Palladium in May 1931. Against the backcloth of a topsy-turvy street scene, with curtseying lamp posts and drunken inns, Max entered, getting the biggest laugh of the night when he explained that his multi-floral suit had cost 'all of two hundred coupons.' One critic noted, 'His ingratiating smile and sure touch proved the truth of the observation that he amuses everyone.'

With three contracts to reappear at the London Palladium and an invitation to do some broadcasting, Max had every right to be pleased with himself as he walked off the stage with a volley of applause only equalled by another bright newcomer, Gracie Fields.

The Times made the observation, 'In variety much depends on a pretty eye for costume, and his green plus-fours were as amusing as his droll chatter and singing. In variety, too, they speed the parting as they welcome the coming turn. Max Miller disappeared into the wings to the strains of Teddy Brown's harmoniously titillated xylophone.'

The professional press threw lavish bouquets at Max; his assurance and unique ability to hold an audience in the palm of his hand frankly amazed the critics. Max Miller had arrived to rescue variety from sinking into the doldrums.

How did Max feel about the show?

'Every artist's ambition is to appear before the King and Queen at a Royal Variety Performance. There's no higher honour in the profession. You can guess what I must have felt like when I got my invitation to give a performance attended by King George V and Queen Mary in the 1931 show.

'Needless to say I was reminded by the variety people that my jokes had to suit the audience. As if I didn't know! Although I'm a bit of a "Cheeky Chappie" on and off the stage, I must admit I felt a bit nervous when I was standing in the wings waiting for my turn to come.

'When I got in front of the footlights I was quite OK. Like any performer in such a show I kept one eye on the audience and one eye on the Royal Box. I'm glad to say I went down well and I've still got a picture in my mind's eye of what went on in the Royal Box after one of my gags.

'I flashed a big diamond ring at the audience, and said, "Eight and a half carat! I got it backing horses. I backed a horse through Woolworth's window."

'Queen Mary leaned back and laughed with the audience. King George must have missed the last few words. He looked a bit puzzled and turned to the Queen as much as to say, what's the joke?

'She whispered to him the tag line and he laughed too! It was a simple little incident but I remember it because of the particular wife who had to repeat to the particular husband what Max Miller said.'

After a week at the Manchester Hippodrome, Max was back at the London Palladium where his salary had jumped to a hundred pounds a week. He was now a named artist who could bring people into a theatre. Drawing power has always been a mystery. Nobody understands why one performer should have it and another not.

Throughout the history of music hall, and later variety, every three or four years has seen the emergence of a new star comedian. He challenges comparison with the old. Is he funnier than other artists or is he merely exploiting his value as a novelty? Fashion seems to have a hand in it, for there are changes in the undertones of our laughter. We are being amused not simply at another man, but at another aspect of our existence.

In 1931 Max consolidated his success. He was found to be good for people's mental balance. It was the time of depression and unemployment. In the act of laughing at this cheeky person, audiences regained their sanity. Max Miller's glorious self-confidence corrected the Freudian theory that self-love is a disease. Max dispelled gloom. There was a bonus. The subject of sex underlined almost every gag he cracked. The expression of indecent ideas was subject to social prohibition, but with Max's way of delivering a dirty story, he never spelt it out, but planted the idea in the audience's imagination. Max dissipated his audience's inhibitions. In control of every facet of his personality, he used the people seated in front of him as the tool of his art.

In the summer during a tour of provincial theatres, Miller played a week at the Pavilion, Glasgow. The response took him down a few pegs. He did not go over so well with audiences north of the Trent, just as northern comedians were not so popular away from their home ground.

In 1931 radio was expanding its potential and the puritanical and educationally-minded Lord Reith found himself forced to cater for popular entertainment. Max Miller was one of the first to climb on the bandwagon. Bryan Michie, who was an effects boy in those days, remembered that Max's style was cramped by the atmosphere of a studio.

'Max Miller was used to playing in enormous variety theatres. To put him cold into a studio with a microphone looming up in front of him was all wrong. He was told to imagine an audience listening to his performance. He replied, "That's not difficult, but I can't work properly unless I get the feedback of laughter. It's an audience that tells me how far to go and what to say next." Max was also worried about keeping to a script. I had an idea he had learned his piece, although he pretended to be reading from the sheets of paper in his hand. Quite frankly, his material was not right for broadcasting. It was the gags from the white book. The great performers on radio wrote specifically for the medium and they put it across in a conversational way. Max relied on a toned-down version of the bang-bang technique he used on the stage.

'Ronald Frankau was a terrific success on radio. By the use of subtle pauses after telling lines, he gave listeners the chance to chuckle to themselves. Max, on the other hand, gabbled away at nineteen to a dozen.

'Things got better for Max on the Saturday Night Music Hall shows produced by John Sharman. I was John's assistant. The BBC let their hair down for the first time. We were given permission to use the famous studio 'Underneath the Arches'. It was presented as near as possible to the real thing, with scenery, costumes, an audience, everything.

'That was just what Max wanted. He came on in that striking costume and played to a receptive audience. Sure enough, in those circumstances, listeners got a measure of Max's magnetic personality. I remember looking round the studio audience. With Max's entrance, everybody sat up in their seats as if to say, "We're going to make the most of this."

'Max stood alone in the 1930s. He possessed enormous vitality —and that's what made him Britain's highest paid variety star. He was prepared to broadcast occasionally because it boosted his popularity in the theatres. Listeners may have missed that mischievous look of his, which suggested his gags were going to be more risqué than they turned out to be but, nevertheless, he became popular over the air. His chirpiness and attack got across.

'Max's chief employer, George Black, was not happy for his artists to be over-exposed on the wireless. Then Max got fed up with the BBC because of the small fees they paid.'

Max's best performances were kept for the theatre which was his living. Because the BBC fee structure was so poor he never bought new material for broadcasting. When Max returned to the London Palladium in October 1931 he amused patrons by carrying a weathercock aloft on an umbrella. He sang a number which began :

> 'My superstition is the weathercock,
> I take it with me everywhere I go.
> I love to see it pointing North
> Or South or even West,
> But when it's pointing East,
> I'm full of woe.'

At the Palladium in January 1932 *The Stage* stated :

'Max Miller is to be congratulated for changing his material. He makes a marked hit early in the bill with his cheeky methods and funny stories.'

Max was principally a London-based comedian and had yet to achieve a nationwide reputation. Mr H Capper recalled his visit to Manchester.

'The year was 1932 and on Shrove Tuesday the students of Manchester University held a Rag Day during which considerable sums of money were extorted from the sometimes unwilling public and given to charity.

'We were allowed into the first house at the Manchester Hippodrome on these occasions free of charge. On that evening the turns were given the traditional bird by the unruly audience.

'Stanelli with his "Hornchestra" had been dismissed with catcalls, a continental artist imitating the noise of a tram had been hooted off, a blowsy contralto had received a few banana skins. In fact, the show was proceeding in excellent Shrove Tuesday style.

'Then a man, unknown to us, appeared on the stage dressed

in a grey bowler hat and pink flowered pyjamas. He started to talk (no microphones of course) amidst the continued hubbub. Then one of our ilk, who was seated near enough to the stage to hear what he was saying, stood up and shouted, "Wait a minute, chaps, this man is good. Give him a chance!" The noise abated sufficiently for a few more to hear the artist. Gradually the whole house of about a thousand was captivated and we were soon rolling in the aisles with laughter.

'After the show, we asked each other who this man was— needless to say it was Max Miller.'

The cinema boom was having a serious effect on variety theatres. Julius Darewski thought it would be a good idea for Max to establish himself overseas, thereby opening doors to engagements for years ahead. It was doubtful if his cockney humour would be acceptable in the USA. The terms offered by Australian managements were disappointing, and Darewski settled for a short tour of South Africa.

Max sailed on the *Balmoral Castle* from Southampton on 22nd April 1932. He described the experience :

'A beautiful cruise, money in my pocket and getting paid for seeing South Africa. It made me a happy bloke, I can tell you. I loved every moment of it. Mind you, I remember shaking in my shoes before my first entrance. I needn't have worried. It could have been the Holborn Empire—the welcome was terrific. My favourite date was the Orpheum in Johannesburg where I was top of the bill in what they called a fifty-fifty show—half variety, half films. They gave me a build-up in the paper called *The Star*, describing me as "the inexhaustible comedian" and "known as England's outstanding mirth-maker".

The Star notice for 17th May 1932 reads :

The Orpheum celebrated its opening as half vaudeville and half cinema entertainment with a lavish programme last night. The audience seemed genuinely glad to get back to the fun of the ' 'alls,' and every vaudeville act was welcomed as an old favourite come home.

The hit of the evening was undoubtably Max Miller, a man attached to a disarming smile. He is one of those rollicking fellows who takes bits of London all over the world and produces them at odd moments to everybody's joy. He sings well and does a step or two of dancing, but the act is chiefly Miller. He told tall stories and when they got taller and taller he smiled more engagingly than ever. His is a pleasing personality of the type Johannesburg takes to its bosom. He should be a rare favourite here.

The words 'marvellous vaudeville' were pasted over the bills and Max was retained for a second week. *The Star* described him as 'a comedian of high ability' and as 'with a style of his own, he is in the front rank of laughter-compelling comedians'.

The Rand Daily Mail was equally enthusiastic. 'Max Miller, "The Cheeky Chappie," topped the vaudeville bill at the Orpheum and supplied much food for laughter and reflection. He has the knack of taking his listeners into his confidence and disarming them with the most intimate stories. His manner is subtle, and his song, "Broken Hearted", was one of the funniest things of the evening.'

Max introduced his 'Hiking' song at Pretoria and after noting the American film, *Devotion*, with Ann Harding, *The Pretoria Daily News* stated :

'Max Miller, The Cheeky Chappie, lives up to his reputation. As a comedian, he has a way of his own. His patter is amusing; his songs, especially one about hiking, are catchy, and his dancing is lively.'

Max arrived at Southampton on 18th July 1932 and that night he opened at the London Palladium and doubled with the Holborn Empire. What a feat ! He was determined to return with a bang. He went down so well the Palladium management engaged him for the Christmas season. The bill was a ministry of all the talents. It included Layton and Johnstone singing their latest hit, 'Love is the Sweetest Thing', and Will Hay in his uproarious school sketch in which his pupils purloined the old man's letters containing their fees. But Max, with a fund of new material, stole the show.

The press had noted the introduction of the guitar first used in accompanying his Hiking song. He sat on a stool, picked up the guitar, and nursing it like a baby, strummed a few chords.

'Like a harp 'in it? Got some volume (another chord). Now

listen . . . (another chord). Get some nice chords on this, can't you—if you know where to put your fingers . . . No . . . we . . el, it's tricky. It's not like a comb, anybody can play a comb . . . all clever stuff I'm givin' you. Miller's the name, lady . . . .there'll never be another, will there? They don't make 'em today, ducks.'

Max abandoned his routine of burlesquing popular singers. He realised the potential of his own particular brand of point number. Max saw an uncharted potential in telling jokes to music.

Just as his jokes were slight so his songs were banal, but how meaningful he made them. The delivery of both songs and patter both followed from the comic flavour of the man. Who else could sing to such effect Sitting on a Star with Sarah?

> 'Sarah, she was getting quite contrary,
> Her wooden leg stuck in the sand—
> I tried to shift it, ain't love grand?
> Got a splinter in my hand—
> Sitting on a star with Sarah.'

or,

> 'Never let a woman wear the trousers,
> Brother, you'll never be free;
> See that she always wears the blouses,
> Take a little advice from me.
> If you're not too careful,
> You'll be standing at the sink
> While she's at the bar,
> buying the boys a drink.'

These songs became a vital part of his act. One in particular became his hallmark. He recollected how it came into being.

'Dozens of song writers sent me numbers. The trouble was, hardly any of them suited my style. I was talking to little Sam Kern in the Express Dairy one day and I told him that I'd hit on a topical idea for a song: "Mary From The Milk Bar."

'Sam said that didn't sound quite right and he suggested "Mary From The Dairy". When I finished the act with "Mary From

The Dairy" it went over better than any number I had featured.
I adopted it as my signature tune.'

> 'I'm known as the Cheeky Chappie,
> The things I say are snappy.
> That's why the pretty girls all fall for me.
> I don't do things contrary
> My love will never vary,
> Ask Mary From the Dairy—
> Here's the key.
>
> I fell in love with Mary From the Dairy,
> But Mary wouldn't fall in love with me;
> Down by an old mill stream
> We both sat down to dream,
> Little did she know that I was thinking of a scheme.
>
> She said let's pick some buttercups and daisies,
> Those buttercups were full of margarine.
> She slipped and we both fell
> Down by a wishing well,
> In the same place where I fell with Nellie Dean.
> "Now on our farm," said Mary From the Dairy,
> "We've got the finest cows you've ever seen.
> I don't do things by halves
> I'll let you see my calves,
> And they're not the same shape calves as Nellie Dean's." '

7   Private Life

MAX MILLER WAS an unsophisticated man and his private life was simple and homely. He had few close friends. He was not a partygoer, never went on a spree and off stage was quiet and unassuming. He enjoyed the company of poor and simple men and women.

He dressed conservatively, and in the West End he wore a quiet brown suit and overcoat, shoes and socks to match, a toning tie and the inevitable homburg.

Max did not cultivate many people in the entertainment business and he was not a member of a professional club.

Miller's image was a ladykilling bounder with his hand up the waitress's skirt. In reality he was almost straightlaced. He was uxorious and domesticated and for him, after the show meant catching the earliest train back to Brighton. This became so much his routine that when he was in a position to bargain the terms of his contracts he had a clause written in which stated that he must be in a position to leave the theatre to catch the last train to Brighton. This was a major concession on the part of managements because it meant that, as top of the bill, he went on early in the second half. When audiences had seen the star, Max, they became bored by sitting through supporting turns until curtain fall.

For an engagement at the Holborn Empire, one act was unable to appear, and Max took the last spot. He was still anxious to reach Victoria station in time, and he did something unheard of in the annals of stage history. At the end of his act, he climbed off the stage into the auditorium, and left the theatre with the patrons by the front of the house.

There was a tradition for a member of the pit orchestra, usually the musical director, to take the artist's band parts to him on his final night, when he received a gratuity, which was shared out with his colleagues.

At the end of Max's starring engagement at the Holborn Empire, Max went into the pit, scooped up his band parts, and with a 'Cheerio boys' he disappeared.

Kathleen gave Max what he never had as a child—security. After nine years of continuous touring, and the horror of indifferent digs, she kept for him a comfortable nest. In 1930 they lived at 2 Princes Terrace, Brighton.

Max had loved his mother, and Kathleen took on the maternal role. She was in many ways a superior person and Max became intimidated by her. However, after almost twenty years of marriage he did find a secret release from her claustrophobic clutches. In the meantime she organised his life with the strictest competence.

On arrival home at night a meal awaited him and each day he would follow the same routine. Max was very conscious of his health; he loved fresh air and exercise. In the summer he went for a daily swim. From the beach he made for the end of the pier and it gave him much satisfaction to climb up and walk back, thus avoiding the price of admittance. When questioned by the pier manager about non-payment, he replied, 'I'm making *you* money—my fans pay to go on the pier to see me.'

In the winter Max liked to cycle along the entire length of the front at Brighton. He continued with his bike until a couple of years before his death. Kathleen would cook him a good lunch, and after an afternoon nap he caught a train to London.

Percy Sargent maintains that Kathleen gave birth to a stillborn baby. In the absence of an object upon which to lavish his affection, Max kept pets. There was a succession of parrots, sometimes five at a time. One, Tony, lived to a great age and there was a budgerigar, Suzy.

At the height of his success Max gave a home to a few carthorses in a paddock attached to his home at Shoreham. He was for ever bringing home stray dogs. One time Kathleen recounted how she found Max's sentimentality had got out of control.

'On that particular night I had not waited up for him. In the early hours of daylight I looked across our bedroom and it appeared as if Max was lying on the bed in his clothes. I got up to discover the dirtiest and biggest black dog I'd ever seen lying across a lovely eiderdown. That was Max all over.'

'Later Max gave a lamb he called Mary the run of the house. She left souvenirs everywhere. Eventually she was taken ill and had to go. When Max was playing the Holborn Empire once he saw a pigeon lying outside the stage door. He picked it up and found it was still breathing. He took it in his dressing room, put in a cardboard box with some cotton wool and fed it with bread and milk. He took it to Brighton and it recovered.

'Max had two parrots called Tony. The first one became ill. On his return from the Holborn Empire that night he said, "How's Tony?" I told him the parrot had died. He was on the verge of tears.

'I knew something else was the matter with him. It appeared two con men had called on him in his dressing room, and talked about an engagement at the National Sporting Club. He accompanied them to the stage door and they saw him put the key to his dressing room on a hook. On his return to his room Max found his salary of forty pounds had been stolen.'

The loss of the parrot compounded his misery. Money meant so much to Max Miller. He became fabled for his meanness which he took to bizarre lengths. He was known to give a porter a penny tip for carrying his bag and he seemed to gain satisfaction from such a petty act. He revelled in his reputation and it became a game of avoiding spending money.

In the war Max purchased a Rolls-Royce. Although petrol rationing was in force, the vendor, as a favour, drove it from Notting Hill Gate to Golders Green Hippodrome where Max was on the bill. The man waited awkwardly for some recompense and Miller grudgingly gave him one shilling. The suggestion that Max did such a thing for publicity, often his own excuse, does not hold water. We have to accept that Max was extraordinarily mean.

An informant rang me at three o'clock in the morning, assured me that he was cold sober and for the next three-quarters of an hour catalogued examples of Max's meanness. He ended by saying, 'To sum it up he was the tightest bastard in Christendom.' It is impossible to gloss over this aspect of Max's character. Not everyone had an axe to grind.

Max resisted with consummate skill ever having to buy drinks. A young comedian was surprised when Max volunteered to meet in the bar for a drink. He was Roy Hudd.

'I was working a double act at the time and we were booked at the Finsbury Park Empire. Max dropped the bombshell on the third night. "Boys, come up to the bar and I'll get you a drink." My mate looked at me—we couldn't believe it—a drink on Max after all we'd heard! Needless to say we went and sat down at a table with Max. A rather embarrassing five minutes followed with no sign of the promised bevy. Eventually I shrugged and asked Max what he wanted. He waved me back to my seat. "Sit down, son, and just wait a minute." Almost at once the doors swung open and in came the audience. It was the interval and they spotted Max straight away. "Oh, Max is here. What'll you have, Max?" Max said, "I'll have a gin and Eddy and Roy, what'll you have?" Max kept his promise. He did get us drinks.'

It was customary for a top-of-the-bill artist to buy the boys of the pit orchestra a drink. When the Cheeky Chappie was on the bill they got their drinks, but only through guile. Max would go into a crowded bar and be surrounded by admirers. One fan would start the ball rolling by saying, 'Tell us one, Max.'

'All right, but it'll cost you.'

'Cost me?'

'Yes, a pint, put it on top of the piano.'

The first gag always went over well and as to be expected, another sucker came forward. 'Tell us another.'

'That's what I like—enthusiasm. I've got fifteen more great gags going for the same price.'

'How come fifteen?'

'There's eleven guys in the pit, there's the chippy, the boy on the spot, the stage manager and the electrician. They'll all want a pint. And if anyone wants two verses of "Mary From The Dairy", that's extra, see? The front of house manager—he only drinks spirits.'

family group. Max Miller in private's uniform (top right) during the 1914–18 war.

x Miller (second from the right) with Jack Sheppard's Entertainers, Brighton, 1919.

Left: 1921 and all that. Th[e]
embryo 'Cheeky Chappie' [in]
the days of 'The Grasshop[per]
Trio'.

Below: Max Miller [and]
Kathleen Marsh rehea[rse]
their variety act, 1922.

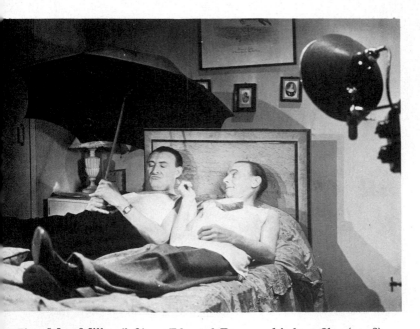

Top: **Max Miller** (left) as *Educated Evans* — his best film (1936).

Bottom: **Max Miller** in his last film, *Asking for Trouble* (1942).

Left: Max Miller on his way to the London Palladium, 1953.

ove: Max Miller entertains in cabaret at Grosvenor House, London, in 1938.

From top: Max Miller on stage: 'Here's a little song beautifully written and beautifully sung.'

'You like me, lady, don't you?'

'What if I am?'

'Splits? No, it hurts me, lady.'

Left: The inimitable 'two book cheeky chappie' in full stage regalia.

Below: 'Max Miller Makes the Queen Roar with Laughter'—so claimed the newspapers at Max Miller's Royal Command Performance in 1950. The royal party is seen in the lower box at the London. Palladium.

Max shortly before he died. This is the last photograph taken of him.

Thus Max would get the drinks lined up on the piano. The fans still loved him. Max had come up the hard way. He had observed how spongers swarmed round the successful pro and it could be fatal to succumb to idle generosity. For Max, money in the bank and future security was paramount. Although he had boundless confidence, he realised that every star is vulnerable. By 1938 he was able to say to Val Parnell, who threatened to black him on the Moss Empires circuit, 'You're thirty thousand pounds too late.'

In Brighton Max indulged in simple pleasures. A stroll along the prom, a few minutes in a pub to see his favourite talking parrot and a chat with Harry Preston was far preferable to the competitive bitchiness of theatrical banter in bars and clubs in London. Anyway, that sort of thing would have been too costly for Max Miller.

For a time Max travelled back to Brighton at night with members of the Crazy Gang. By arrangement, whosoever left the train last paid for the drinks at the bar. The boys found Max was ducking his turn so they decided to play a trick on him. They bribed the driver to slow down at Preston Park station, enabling them to jump out. The train then accelerated to the next stop, Brighton, leaving Max to settle the biggest account of the week.

Three categories of people can attest to Max Miller's generosity—down and outs, the blind and criminals. In several interviews he was quoted as saying, 'I've known what it's like to be hungry.' The poverty of his childhood and the influence of his shiftless father imbued him with a sympathy for the underdog, and his wife tried to restrain him from helping such people.

Kathleen managed Max's affairs and held the reins tight. She was a saving woman with pretentions of gentility. A former cleaner mentioned how thrifty she was, giving as an excuse the uncertainty of her husband's profession. She was shocked by some of Max's acts. In notes she has written about her husband she may have exaggerated his good qualities. She talks of how he would shower money on every tramp he passed; how he would stop his car and put a wounded animal out of its misery.

Over Max's generosity Kathleen suggests an air of 'tut tut'. She recounts how one day 'We were golfing in a bitterly cold wind. I had knitted for Max a very nice helmet to keep his ears warm, which he was wearing for the first time. The sight of a shivering old tramp was too much for Max. I hadn't spotted him. He left me abruptly and then came back, saying, "Have you got ten bob on you?" I had and gave it to Max. Off he went and he came back in that biting wind minus his beautiful warm helmet, which had taken me hours and hours to make, at a considerable cost, especially for him. He'd given it to the tramp! That was typical of Max!'

For the blind Max had a constant sympathy. This stemmed from his nightmarish experience during the First World War when he temporarily lost his sight for three days. He said, 'People talk about my lovely blue eyes. I thank God I can see with them every day of my life.'

Max's greatest act of charity was to loan his mansion at Ovingdean to St Dunstan's for the duration of the war. It was used as an annex to the hospital.

Hilda M Barnett wrote :

'My brother, who was the same age as Max, was blind and he had to lie flat on a spinal carriage. I brought him to Woodingdean at the beginning of the war.

'Max had tears in his eyes when he was introduced to us and he said, "To think you've been lying on your back all these years. I'll give you ten shillings a week for the duration of your life."

'I once asked Max about his act and he said, "The public asks for what I give them, but it's not really me."

'Max visited us many times. God bless his memory.'

Miller was introduced to a blind pianist, Alfred Thripp, at Boscombe by Roy Denton, who recalled Max saying :

'He's always cheerful, yet he's blind. I'm going to get him work on my bills.'

Max experienced opposition from several managements who were against booking anybody with a handicap—they considered it bad for business to play on sympathy. Max even wrote a song to fit Alfred : "Isn't It Grand To See Someone Smile?" He gave Alfred work for some seven years—not all the time—because Max wasn't appearing frequently.

In 1939 Miller's gift of a hundred pounds to the Whitehawk

Private Life

Canteen funds in Brighton received wide publicity. It was a place of refuge for poor children. At a ceremony Max was quoted as saying, 'I used to go without a meal when I had nothing better to do than play in the streets around here.'

Max had 'arrived' by the 1930s and with cash in hand in excess of thirty thousand pounds, he was advised to invest in property. He bought an impressive, three-storey mansion called Woodland Grange at Ovingdean, near Brighton. It was formerly the home of Mrs Van der Elst, who achieved notoriety for her anti-hanging campaign.

Max took a personal interest in maintaining the grounds, and he began new hobbies of gardening and bricklaying. Riding became another pastime and he hired a mount for a canter over the Downs on Sunday mornings.

Colonel A G H Dukes wrote about an incident in 1939.

'I was ferreting rabbits in the grounds of Max's home at Ovingdean, when I came face to face with him. The conversation went something like this :

' "What are you doing?"

' "Catching your rabbits, Mr Miller."

' "Oh, are they mine? Show me how it's done."

'At the end of the day I was invited to supper when the caretaker said the main dish was roast veal. A week later the caretaker told me he'd served "young badger". Max, I'm sure, didn't know!'

When Max lived in Princes Terrace he rented a basement flat to George Meachen who occupied it from 1930 onwards with his wife and daughter. His son was born there. Meachen idolised his landlord and he did many useful things for a nominal reward.

'I'd paint his shoes twice a week and renew the studs on the soles for his tap dancing. The studs were in different colours including red, blue and yellow, to show up to the audience, and from the front they looked very effective. I also copied out his band parts.

'Mr Miller was a totally different man off stage. He was very quiet and dignified. He would rehearse his songs and jokes to me. I made a cockerel for him, secured on the spokes of an umbrella. I took material to a small tailor's shop in Brighton where his stage suits were made up for him.

99

'People would mob Max as he walked along the sea front. Others would knock on the front door and some asked for money.

'Maxholme was his next house on the seafront. Then he lived at the Cresta Hotel, also on the seafront. Then he moved into Woodland Grange, formerly owned by Mrs Van der Elst, who had an interest in the Zeekol Soap Company.

'I remember a time when Max had a nasty cold. He was due to open at the Brighton Hippodrome. I gave his chest a thorough good rub. He soon got better. I used to take his meal to the theatre and then he'd allow me to watch his performance from the wings.

'My biggest thrill was to see him off to London when he was playing at the Holborn Empire or the Palladium.'

Max's chief hobby was golf. He had the skill of a professional. If a stranger, who knew nothing of his ability, asked him for a game, Max would say, 'I'll play you for a dozen new balls.' Max never bought golf balls. Riding was another pursuit which started when he received tuition for an appearance in a film.

Despite strings of offers which could have kept him constantly occupied, Kathleen persuaded him to join her on a Mediterranean cruise, and the couple also fulfilled an ambition by touring Germany.

Julius Darewski advised Max against going to Germany.

'Listen, Maxie. You look so Jewish they might throw you in a concentration camp.'

'Hitler daren't touch me,' said Max. 'He knows that George Black would sue him if I failed to turn up for my next date at the Palladium.'

Max was fascinated by crime. He often attended Brighton Quarter Sessions and he cultivated the Recorder. To him a visit to Lewes Assizes was better than paying for a seat at the pictures. If he felt sorry for an old person up for petty larceny he would wait outside and give the person the sum of money handed over to the court. Sir James Cassels, who invited Max to his chambers, and took him out to lunch, warned him that the majority of people he helped were not deserving.

In March 1939 Max was fined one pound for driving an unlicensed car at Lewes. A policeman said when he drew attention to the expired licence, he replied, 'I have so many dates to remember I must have overlooked it.' In a letter to the court Max said, 'I was filming at the time and my mind was on my work to the exclusion of everything else.'

After the war Max sold Woodland Grange for £7,000. He bought an impressive house near Shoreham-on-sea called Kingston Buci. There were four acres of grounds. The Millers moved in during March 1946. Kathleen was quoted in the *Evening News*:

'We have been looking for ten years for a house we felt we could settle in. We wanted something near Brighton and by the sea, with trees, flowers and room to grow vegetables. Max likes pottering—pulling things down, sawing trees, digging and tinkering with his car. He wants scope and the new house will provide that.'

As the costs began to mount Max began selling vegetables to greengrocers in Brighton. The house was too small to be used as a club, another of his ideas, and eventually he sold out in favour of a flat—4 Portland Mansions on Marine Parade.

Kathleen Miller developed ideas of grandeur. Although she enjoyed the affluence that Max's earning capacity allowed her, she did not like her husband's image as a ribald variety artist. Off stage she suppressed Max's natural exuberance so successfully he was reduced to a quiet, thinking man, given to long silences. In a press interview Kathleen showed herself as a woman given to more tolerance than was really the case.

'Max is unpractical in the house, but he does try. Once, just before a dinner party, he fused all the lights by a sudden decision to change the wiring system. On another occasion, he sawed off the legs of a Queen Anne bed and fitted iron casters. "Look," he said, "you can move it around now."

'Max is still a boy at heart, always himself and completely natural.

'I remember asking him to make a special effort to impress some important guests at a dinner party. Max trying to talk prunes and prisms was so awful, I told him never to do it again.

'I dislike the publicity that fame brings my husband, and the interruptions it makes in our private life. I've often wished Max was able to come home at normal hours. I'd see more of him then.'

That opinion was shared by Max Miller until the late 1930s when he felt the need to break the bonds and lead part of his life away from his wife's constant supervision.

8   Stardom 1932–1945

IN 1933 MAX WAS busy with his film career, playing supporting parts. Although not topping the bill he had become a regular favourite at the Palladium besides many provincial and suburban dates. Julius Darewski no longer had to sell him but had to juggle with the many offers that came his way.

Darewski urged Max to spend money on new material. 'I know it's against your inclinations, Max, but put your hand in your pocket, if you want to keep progressing.' Nightly, at the stage door, down-at-heel gag merchants sold him new variations of old chestnuts. Max also spent much time in the Express Dairy where all the Tin Pan Alley rejects were hummed over for his approval. Occasionally Max made a discovery—and only he could bring shine to such material as 'I'm One of Nature's Greatest Gifts to Women'. If Max thought he was on to a winner the composer would suggest going to a rehearsal room to play it over.

'Listen, mate,' said Max. 'It ain't Chopin. We'll pop into the Excelsior pub and you can thump it out on the old Joanna for free.' Max found a few winners with the minimum of expenditure.

In January 1933 he was at the Victoria Palace where he appeared in a golfing suit. Starting with a vocal item he delved into his blue and white books containing an inexhaustible supply of gags. The use of the white book for clean gags and the blue one for the suggestive ones was later to become part of his stock-in-trade. The books of course were empty.

From the Victoria Palace to the Palladium in February. April found him at the Holborn Empire with a new song, 'One Fell By the Water Fall', and a spasm on the miniature xylophone. By public demand he was back again within a month.

Those were the days of the big bands. In June 1933 Max was at the Palladium with Duke Ellington. For his return in August, it was Jack Hylton's turn. Max had comic competition from Lily Morris—'Why Am I Always the Bridesmaid and Never the Blushing Bride?' and 'Don't Have Any More Mrs Moore'—and Nat Mills, for ever saying, 'Let's get on with it' to his miserable better half, Bobbie. The irascible Will Hay was also on top form.

Hugh James, the musical director, already quoted when he met Max at the Putney Hippodrome in the 1920s, moved to the Shepherd's Bush Empire.

'Max was by then an established artist. He was very tight with money. During his week at Shepherd's Bush, I saw him in the bar of the pub next door and I invited him to have a drink with me. "Yes," said Max. "I'll have a pint." He did not return the compliment before I left and returned to the orchestra pit.

'At rehearsal, Max asked me if I could play some suitable storm music whilst he ran across the stage carrying an umbrella. I told him I had a suitable orchestration, which, if he liked, I would sell to him for the price of a pint of beer.

'After the first house on the opening Monday night, Max sent for me and I went to his dressing room. He said, "I like the storm music, Hugh. You said I could have it for the cost of a pint, eightpence. Here's a shilling, have you got fourpence change?"

'I might say, if he had gone to an arranger, it would have cost him over a pound.

'The next time I met Max I was conducting at the Chelsea Palace. At the band call, he asked me if the orchestra would 'busk' his intro : "Mary From The Dairy". I informed him that an artist earning the money he was could afford to buy a set of band parts. I have always objected to my orchestra busking. Everyone plays different harmonies and notes, and the result is chaos. He didn't like me for what I had said, but the next day he did provide me with the proper orchestration.'

Robert W Dennis wrote to tell me he saw Max at the New Cross Empire.

'I shall always remember his ladylike stroking of his right eyebrow; then he gave a perfect pause, followed by "Well, what if I am?"'

'One of his best gags was: "There were eight women in a boat and one was expecting a happy event. The other seven wanted to help her, but they were all in the same boat."'

'Max went into a nearby pub between houses and he entertained the customers if they bought him a pint. He told us this one: "A chappie on the stage wrote the letter F on a blackboard. He called up a man from the audience and he asked him what letter he had written up. The man said K. 'That's funny,' said this chappie. 'When I write F *you see* K' "'

It was at the Finsbury Park Empire that Max caused the house manager to be fined £5 for allowing this gag to be cracked: 'Have you heard about the girl of eighteen who swallowed a pin, but didn't feel the prick until she was twenty-one?'

Although the critics had noted Max's goldmine of material, it was impossible with so many engagements in the West End to maintain originality. He went some way towards conquering this problem with his rapport with the audience. Certain expressions became part of his *sine qua non*. He was saying, 'There's never going to be another' thirty years before he finished the game. 'Shut up . . . yes, sh . . ut up. We . . ll . . . we . . ll. You filthy lot. You're the sort that gets me a bad name Listen . . . listen,' suggested that he was the puritan, and the wicked thoughts were in the minds of his listeners.

In January 1934 at the Palladium 'Max leered at the audience as they howled at his audacity'. There again a month later his act was at the opposite pole to Ethel Barrymore, whose quiet style was a failure in that little masterpiece from the pen of J M Barrie —*The Twelve Pound Look*. At the Holborn Empire Max entered on the back of a prop camel. It was unusual for him to be topped in the naughtiness stakes, but G S Melvin outdid his rival by recounting the exploits of the 'Lisle Street Ladies'. But at the Holborn Empire in November *The Stage* noted that 'his cheeky songs and jokes were never better appreciated'.

Variety turns fell into several categories. Some made the

audience abandon itself to happy thoughtless laughter; there was the act that filled them with breathless admiration at physical strength and dexterity; at other times they were asked to wallow in sentimentality. These reactions were constant, but with the coming of proper education, the cinema and the radio, changes were evolved in the manifestations that evoked them. The red-nosed comic had almost disappeared by 1934. Comedians had to be funny rather than just look funny. Not that low comedy's day was done; it had to be low in a subtler, more refreshing way. Time was when an artist like Max Miller would not have got engagements in the straight make-up he affected. True, his costume was mildly eccentric, but his visual appeal lay rather in his friendly normal face.

Two *Times* notices for appearances at the Holborn Empire in 1935 summed up the impact of Max's act; in May he was the success of the evening.

'Even when the jokes he made were not particularly good, his manner, his intimacy with the audience persuaded them "it was all good stuff, lady". He entered in an incredible suit of black and yellow stripes and there was a lot of talk just about Max. Although he is a single turn, the essence of Max demanded it. Instead of another actor feeding him the audience did the job for him.

In November 1935 he was the crowd puller.

'Arthur Tracy, an abandoned sentimentalist, was on the bill. It was a relief to see Max Miller, the Cheeky person, who forestalls the laughter of the audience before he makes a joke. He buttonholes the audience in his own intimate way and asks them to listen. Having got the ear and the applause, he, with a deprecating hand, admonishes them for having lured him on to tell his funny tales.'

By September 1936, the patrons of the Holborn Empire welcomed a master of his craft.

'A friendly bond has to exist between a music-hall performer and his audience. Although they may glitter, coldness and distance are taboo. In the art of intimacy Max Miller is a past master. He does not need a microphone. Standing on the edge of the stage he seemed to be amongst his audience and if the indecorous things he pretends to see there are more funny than probable, laughter was all.'

Max added fresh touches to his patter and business to give an air of spontaneity. At the Chiswick Empire in February 1936 he provided a criticism of his own act as he went along—it wasn't critical of course, rather a running commentary in felicitousness. Filming for long periods he fitted in as many London dates as possible, including the Empires at Shepherd's Bush, Finsbury Park and Penge.

In 1937 Miller was continuously engaged, mainly in London. He was attaining the peak of success and to mention all the theatre receptions only adds to a repetition of accolades. His favourite venue was the Holborn Empire where standing-room only notices were outside night after night. Supporting turns included Vic Oliver, the Western Brothers, Kenneth and George, public school cads, and Dick Henderson who 'Tip Toed Through the Tulips'. Max constantly introduced new gags and for one engagement he gave admirers three new numbers, 'Waste Not, Want Not', 'The Singing Master' and 'Rambling Roses'. He also suggested the awful implications of 'La-di-da-di-da', an irresistible refrain. He buttonholed his audience in the agreeable manner of a man on the friendliest terms with the world. When pleasantly sentimental, he serenaded 'Sally' in words that had no subtlety and in a voice which had no obvious breaks he showed he possessed the elusive attraction of a unique personality.

Max was largely based in London through the 1930s and his earning capacity increased with every year that passed. Less successful artists who relied on provincial and suburban engagements found their frequency of employment was diminished. Variety managements were fighting a losing battle with cinemas, the choice of the masses, which were cheaper and more comfortable.

Variety theatres kept open by presenting twice-nightly revues, straight plays and musicals, and road shows, which usually consisted of a star heading a variety bill which went on tour.

Wireless kept thousands of people indoors, though occasionally the trend was reversed, and broadcasting stars made personal appearances on the halls, and the ones who could project in a theatre became box-office attractions.

The pianist Charlie Kunz had a tremendous following on the air. At the Glasgow Empire, an Irish comedian, Sam Rayne, had to follow Kunz. Rayne tried to start his patter but the house refused to listen to him. They merely chanted, 'We want Charlie! We want Charlie!' After five minutes of trying to make himself heard, Rayne said, 'Well, if you bloody well want Charlie I'll get him.' He walked off the stage, got Kunz from his dressing room, the piano was pushed on the stage, and he did another impromptu performance for ten minutes.

When Max Miller played a provincial date, the house was often booked to capacity before he opened. Quite often a large percentage of the audience would stay in the bar until Max's act was due. It was because of this that Max began to make guest appearances during the running time of other acts, which he continued to do until the end of his career. Max would join in with a song and dance act, try his hand at juggling and play unexpected characters—especially those requiring a special costume. Max as a ploughboy, a policeman or a bad trumpet player in immaculate dress clothes was sure of a laugh.

The juggler, Billy Gray, described one night at the Holborn Empire.

'Max was a riot that night. He just went on and on and the audience wouldn't let him go. He overran his time so much the stage manager brought the house tabs down on him.

'Unfortunately for Max, Val Parnell was out front. I was standing in the wings as Parnell came storming through the pass door, his face as black as thunder. "You'll never work the Moss Empires again as long as you live!" he stormed.

' "Mr Parnell," said Max, "you're thirty thousand pounds too late." '

True enough Max was barred for some time. He had to get his agent Julius Darewski to book him in the opposition houses, and where they didn't exist he'd even work a cinema. The proprietors were only too happy to give up films for a week to welcome a big draw like Max Miller.

'Max packed 'em in everywhere and in doing so, killed the business at the Moss Empire dates. You've got to be a great performer to do that.

'George Black had to let Parnell have his way for a few weeks to save his face, but on business considerations he was soon over-ruled, and Max was back topping the bills at the Holborn Empire, the Palladium and all the Moss Empire dates.

'Max was unpredictable—I think he even surprised himself sometimes. I worshipped the man and when I was on a bill with him I'd always try and watch his act. I remember slipping into a side seat in the stalls of the New Cross Empire. Max was in great form that night. He cracked some brand new gags.

' "I've got a great ambition," said Max. "I'd like to work in France. To be a star in Paris for instance. I'd look outside the theatre and see my name up there in great big French letters."

'For a moment there was silence. Cold perspiration poured out of me. Then there was one hell of a laugh.'

The distinguished dramatic critic James Agate made an attempt to analyse the secret of Max's success.

'Let it be said right away that the whole of Max Miller's material is unpardonable and not to be condoned on any pretext whatsoever. But the manner of its delivery is also unblushing, and it is this which is its justification, as it is with Rabelais. How right Burke was to say that vice by doubling its grossness loses half its evil! A dirty mind, as somebody remarked, is a perpetual feast. This, one admits, is the plaguey, moral point of view. Considered as a piece of acting the performance is a miracle of wit and timing. For twenty minutes or so, you sit and listen to the kind of thing with which the rogues in Beaumarchais' world might be supposed to entertain the scamps in Molière's. It is also rather like the kind of confidences Mr Smauker might have imparted to Mr Tuckle and indeed to the table generally, after that "*wulgar* beast" Harris had left.

'It is just a little difficult to "place" this grotesque socially. At times the character which Mr Miller so brilliantly assumes suggests a cockney behind his barrow. Or he is of the light-fingered persuasion, thimble-rigger and card sharper. Or like Petticoat Lane on a Sunday morning. Sometimes his aura is Mayfair's, and you dream that night-club touts must be like this. Perhaps Prince of Cheap-Jacks might be the best description—with this difference, that the actor is never cheap, since there is intelligence behind every word that he utters. And he utters them so well that every man-Jack in the audience laughs his fill.'

In an attempt to broaden his appeal Max flirted with cabaret throughout the 1930s. Despite his stock-in-trade, putting over his material with an air of intimacy, Max needed a big audience with a corresponding reaction, to be fully successful. The exception was the Trocadero, where in October 1935 he scored heavily. There was the same audience that filled the Holborn Empire and the Palladium, ordinary folk of limited means. The sophisticates of the Café de Paris demanded humour that brought their intellect into play.

One day Max gave an impromptu lunchtime performance at the famous Daly's Theatre in Leicester Square. With no roof above his head, and the stage piled high with debris, including the remnants of the footlights, he sang 'Mary From the Dairy' to a crowd of demolition workers and other onlookers. Max was making capital out of a sad occasion. The theatre, which had seen some of the best loved musical shows, was being pulled down to make way for the new Warner Cinema. Max's film, *Thank Evans*, was due to open there.

Max Miller was invited to appear in his second Royal Variety Performance at the Palladium on 15th November 1937. He adorned himself more extravagantly than ever with a vividly-coloured dressing gown and a coat trimmed with red, white and blue silk.

'I know how to dress for the occasion, nice and quiet.'

The house roared with laughter and immediately he dispersed any gravity that still may have lurked there. Everybody found his humour was easy to understand and appreciate.

'A tramp stopped a woman and said, "I haven't eaten for five days." "Well, my good man," she said, "you'll have to force yourself." The other day a motorist ran over a cat. "This will kill my wife," said the owner. "Well, don't let her eat it," said the motorist.'

Max described the show.

'I had ten minutes and at the rehearsal I rattled off as many gags as I could. George Black said, "Slow it down, Max. Not so fast on the night!"

' "Very well, guv'nor."

' "And no 'blimeys' please."

' "Yes, guv'nor."

'But I'm afraid I couldn't resist the temptation to quicken my delivery as my act got under way. I started to tell the gag about the sailor who arrived home, and who banged on the front door with a cricket bat. Then he raced to the back door. Half way through I wondered if I should carry on. I stopped and I said, "No, not tonight. Any other night, but not tonight."

'While the audience was laughing, I glanced up to the Royal Box and I saw that everything was going well too. So I finished the story.

'Was I nervous? Well, let me tell you what happened. Before I went on I saw George Formby and he looked pretty pale.

' "Don't be nervous."

' "Well, what about yourself?" said George.

' "I'm fine."

'After the show, there was a party in a hotel. I found I was carrying a coat-hanger, which I'd been holding for two hours. I must have been nervous.'

In 1938 Max tried out new material at the Finsbury Park Empire and the New Cross Empire, before he returned to a great welcome at the Palladium in July. His act was so strong it was held over a second week. Hearty laughter showed that the house adored his cheeky humour, and a couple more Palladium dates were offered for late July and in August. Whereas, early on, when playing for George Black, he was one of three artists who shared top billing, a clever innovation by this thinking impresario, now Max was there, alone, the star of the programme.

Max was interviewed about his radio career.

'People say I was not on the radio so much in 1937. I'm under contract to George Black, and he's not keen on his artists broadcasting too much. He says it discourages people going to the theatre. I decided to do a double act on the radio, so I teamed up with my wife again. We called ourselves "Mr and Mrs Sargent". The act was a husband and wife's slanging match and there were some pretty sharp words flying about. Listeners' letters poured into Broadcasting House. People recognised my voice and some of them said, I "bamboozled the public". I did it for a joke.'

After the Palladium season Max fell ill with lumbago and

bronchitis and it was not until October that he was fit enough to reappear at the Holborn Empire where he received a royal welcome.

In February 1939 Max was involved in a heated backstage dispute during his appearance at the Birmingham Hippodrome. Max described what happened.

'I had been using the gag all the week and I held that it was mine. It was ten years old, but twisted around a bit. Another artist complained that it was his gag and there was a good deal of trouble and argument. I got so upset on Saturday—and I was running a temperature of 102 degrees—that I could not carry on. I had to go home to Brighton to be fit to open at the London Adelphi the next Monday.'

Early in 1939 four West End theatres were given over to light entertainment, and George Black presented Max Miller at the Adelphi, heading a strong bill with Florence Desmond, who was in his last Palladium season. Max packed the house and was retained for a second week, which meant doubling with the Finsbury Park Empire, where his fans were loath to see him go each night and he was booked to go back in October. A return to the Palladium in July was sandwiched between four visits to the Holborn Empire. *The Times* made some interesting comments on his first appearance there that year.

'Mr Max Miller, who is appearing at the Holborn Empire, recently had his performance recorded for the gramophone, It is a medium more sympathetic to this performance than cold print can ever be, since, as with all variety turns that do not depend on technique, the critic is continually at a loss to record the peculiar effect Mr Miller achieves with a smile and a wink and a glance round the stalls. It is the kind of accomplishment not to be gauged until the comedian is added to the repertoire of the mimic, and even then one would possibly have to fall back on that word of evasive, shifting meaning—character. In this case, character has the most valuable of meanings in the music hall, warmth and intimacy and the cheerfulness, so that we believe the tables are turned and it is the comedian who pays for the pleasure of seeing a familiar audience.'

Two months later, in April 1939, *The Times* stated :

'There are a number of popular and familiar faces at the

Holborn Empire this week, and prominent among them is that of the glinting and persuasive Mr Max Miller. Mr Miller is a sartorial outrage, and a man must have a way with him before he could bring himself to don such deplorable garments. Mr Miller has that way. He is the most intimate of all comedians, and he makes the audience feel that the footlights and the width of the space that divides him from the auditorium are an absurd and outmoded convention. In spirit he is in the next seat to everyone, nudging them confidentially, an amiable, adaptable, slightly disconcerting companion.'

In 1939 Max began a two-year stint for the *Sunday Dispatch*, providing a page of gags every week.

'I'd tell you the story of the red hot poker, only I don't think you'd grasp it.

'That reminds me of the chorus girl who married a rich old invalid. She promised to take him for better or worse. She really took him for worse, but he got better.

'As I always say, lady, some girls are like flowers. They grow wild in the woods.'

'The missus said to me yesterday, "Every time you see a pretty girl, you forget you are married." "No," I told her, "I remember."

'I saw a girl who was proud of her figure. Just to make conversation I asked her, "What would you do if a chap criticised your figure?" "Well," she said, "I wouldn't hold it against him."

'Two girls were talking on a bus. "Are you wearing those lovely new undies?" "No, I'm saving them." "For a rainy day?" "No, for a windy day."

'Dora went swimming the other day and sat on a broken bottle on the beach. She went to the doctor who said, "Where is the injury?" Well, doctor," said Dora. "I'll show you if you promise not to look."

'A pal of mine married his typist. They get along just the same as before. When he dictates to her she takes him down.

'My young nephew, Roland, was having a lesson in grammar and his teacher wrote down on the blackboard, "I didn't have no fun at the seaside." She turned round and said, "Roland, how should I correct that?" "Get a boy friend," he told her.

'I bumped into a girl in the blackout. "Sorry, ducks." "Don't mention it." "Pleased to meet you." "The same to you," she giggled. "Listen, ducks, haven't I met you some place before?" "I think so, your face feels familiar." '

Max used gags from this series for radio broadcasts in the 1950s.

Although Max relied on these sort of quips for his stage act, he often used visual gags as well. He would start a spectacular demonstrations of the splits, and then, half way down, he'd say, 'First half first house; second half second house' (Or tomorrow if it *was* the second house!)

John A Boardman remembered Max at the Metropolitan :

'Max had a cardboard box slung round his neck; it was of the kind used by civilians to carry their gas masks. Max's saucy blue eyes scanned the ladies in the audience and he waggled the box up and down. Then, in his inimitable way he said, 'I haven't got my gas mask in here, lady.'

'He paused for a moment as if to defy the ladies to guess what he had got in the box. Then he continued :

' "No . . . it's not . . . it's Hitler's secret weapon."

'There were some chuckles. "Shall I show you? Shall I?"

'Max opened the box and took out a long pink sausage. It looked as if it could have been a pink sausage; it might well have been something else. I never heard Max get a bigger laugh.'

By December 1939 Miller had reached a turning point in his career. He was at the top and there was only one way he could go—downhill. The process took five years. Meanwhile, as Britain's favourite variety star, his act was in danger of over-exposure. His experience in films proved he could not characterise well. He was trapped by his own creation of 'The Cheeky Chappie'.

Revue was the only thing left. By appearing in the same show for a season, Max was relieved of the difficulty of finding new material. Sketches allowed him to adapt the dialogue to suit himself. George Black, born on the same day as Adolf Hitler, saw a glaring juxtaposition in Lord Haw-Haw and Max Miller, hence his show *Haw Haw* for the Holborn Empire which opened in December 1939 and ran until the end of July 1940.

To George Black, who personally produced the show, the thought of Haw-Haw's regimented voice having the slightest connection with the endearing, confidential vulgarities of Miller had a delicious fantasy about it. Unfortunately the sketches were slight and deficient in wit and a critic wrote the obvious : 'To force Max Miller to speak to others on the stage is a mistake. He needs to work as a solo artist and it is only then he shows his genius for manipulating an audience.'

The name of Fred Shuff used to be well known as a writer of touring revues. He fell on bad times and wrote to Max who was looking for new material for *Haw Haw* and suggested a couple of gags. Max took the gags and Shuff too. This wizened, comical little fellow appeared in a race course and a dugout scene. The dugout scene was the only Army sketch in the history of the theatre to be presented without one mention of a sergeant-major. Max was proud of that. Max appeared as an old, old soldier. So old that he once slept in Anne Boleyn's bed. And he had one of Wellington's cannon balls pickled in gin. His tin hat was a halo to his cherubic chops.

In another scene Max was Hitler, complete with moustache and lock and, of course, he had his flowered suit and white homburg for a scene as The Cheeky Chappie—'All clever stuff, lady.'

Haw Haw was loud and rude and chirpy. There were can-can girls, Bebe Daniels and Ben Lyon in song and sketch, and the genius of Gaston Palmer, a juggler who missed his tricks on purpose.

Encouraged by the box-office success of *Haw Haw*, George Black set about staging a more ambitious revue for Max called *Apple Sauce* which opened at the Holborn Empire in August 1940. It was well up to the boisterous, roystering, make-and-keep-it-snappy standard of its predecessor. Max, who appeared in several sketches, was the clown in chief, with clever impersonations from Doris Hare as Mistinguett and Afrique as Churchill and Caruso singing 'The Lost Chord'.

To audiences of 1940 Max Miller was like a debauché of the Restoration stage. His anecdotes and apophthegms would have suited the toughest audience from that far from tender age. The idiom was his own, and in print it reads as tame stuff by today's standards. However, an artist in *Apple Sauce*, Doris Hare, summed up Max's impact in the show.

'Delivered with that roll of the eye, that mastery of timing and mischievous insinuation, his patter captured any audience not prone to blushing. Even an audience who found *Apple Sauce* somewhat flagging, and short of music-hall relish. Enter Max and all was well.

'Max was a great comedian. The cumulative effect of one gag after another was to send some people into hysterics. He had enormous sex appeal, and women would literally writhe in their seats just looking at him. For want of another word, he exerted an almost mesmeric influence. He'd do a few rudimentary steps and they thought he was a dancer; he would tinkle at the piano and they were under the impression he could play—he couldn't; his power was so great he'd even get the people thinking what he was saying was fresh and fragrant!

'Max was always looking for new material. He had an upright piano in his dressing room, and he would often call me in to give an opinion of a song or a gag.

'I remember the stage door keeper at the Holborn Empire used to stand outside and watch the bombs dropping in distant parts of London. One night a bomb dropped on the theatre, and we closed prematurely.'

Max Miller started rehearsals for *Apple Sauce* uncertain of how to give the public a fresh image. He had returned to the Café de Paris in January 1940, where, despite a first-night audience including Beatrice Lillie, Leonora Corbett, Tommy Farr and A A Milne, he was not a success. In *Apple Sauce* he appeared as a member of the Home Guard, a man in evening dress and as a fugitive, but, as always, he was only his true self when he was alone with the audience, using his amazingly self-confident technique.

The stage and screen actress Jean Kent was nineteen and using the name Jean Carr when she was engaged for the chorus of *Apple Sauce*. She recalled the show.

'Max had a woman to feed him in the sketches but he wasn't happy with the way she handled her parts.

'I was bright eyed and bushy tailed and I sat in the stalls throughout rehearsals. One day the producer, Charles Henry, who was working under the direction of George Black, said, "You know all these sketches, don't you?"—"Yes"—"Well, you're on."

'Max wasn't a bit pleased, but when things began to shape well, he was kind to me. He wasn't easy to work with—on the first night he was panic-stricken. Even when the show had been running some time, he'd wander off the script, and I had to lead him back to get the pay-off gag across. On other occasions he tried something entirely new, and I had to guess what the feed lines should be.

'One night he was particularly annoyed with the BBC. They wanted him to do a broadcast, but had returned his script. They didn't like some of the material, including the joke about how to drink a cocktail and what to do with the cherry. Instead of doing his usual routine, he spent twelve minutes tearing a strip off the BBC and the house was falling about with laughter.

'I rate variety artists higher than legitimate actors. I was brought up in that line of the profession. Variety artists, Max Miller included, tended to be down to earth. Straight actors have stars in their eyes and they inhabit a world that doesn't exist for anybody else.

'Max made it look easy to hold an audience; nothing is easy for a performer. Max loved his work. He had enormous vitality, an essential ingredient for a comedian, it gives magnetism. Max gauged the temperature of an audience and had wonderful timing. He once gave me some good advice : "When in doubt, wait." In other words, if you wait long enough, the laugh will come. Other artists have tried to ape his style—but that's an impossibility—he was right when he said, "There'll never be another."

'Max wasn't filthy. He'd start a gag with only one possible dénouement—then he'd pause, and the audience would do the rest. Max would say, "You wicked lot," which was very unfair. His songs gave balance to his act; they had a poignant charm.

'I remember one sketch in *Apple Sauce* which took place on the Thames Embankment. Max was dressed immaculately in evening clothes and he spoke to me.

' "Would you like a cigarette?"

' "No thank you. I don't smoke."

'Max produced a hip flask from his pocket : "Have a drink."

' "No thank you. I don't drink."

' "Well, how about a kiss then?"

' "No thank you !"

117

' "Don't smoke, don't drink, don't kiss," said Max. "You're not fit to live with"—whereupon he pushed me into the Thames.

'Max taught me more about playing comedy than anybody else. The only artist who came near him was Leslie Henson—he was entirely different, his comedy derived from characterisation.'

When *Apple Sauce* had to close at the Holborn Empire, George Black engaged Max for a nine-week season at the Brighton Hippodrome, which was repertory revue—a different programme each week, with sketches from *Apple Sauce* and other George Black shows. Max was his radiant self and the *Brighton and Hove Herald* of 28th September 1940 gave him generous praise.

'Max pops in and out between the turns and is, so to speak, the life and soul of it all. Now in a lounge suit, now in pyjamas of unbelievable hue, now in an overcoat no other man could have, he has the audience with him every moment. That cheeky air, that infectious laugh, that eloquent flash of the eyes, all so typical of Max, make up a potent tonic for the times. Perhaps the secret weapon behind it all is the pause. No other comedian knows the value of the pause so perfectly as Max. Not that his pauses are long—they are brief, as a matter of fact—but they are just long enough to open up an avenue of speculation between the saucy question and the innocuous answer and all the way through Max's wonderful smile was there to keep things going.'

Jean Kent visited Max's home in Brighton. 'Charming—except for the frightful smell of the parrots. That was the time when I grew to know Max well. Off the stage he was a quiet man with an almost innocent sense of humour. He loved shaggy dog stories. I remember one about two babies meeting in the park. One said :

' "I'm a girl."

' "I'm a boy."

' "How do you know?"

' "I've got blue booties on."

'Max had a reputation for meanness. He didn't buy drinks for an enormous procession of hangers-on who professed to know him, and pounced on him in bars. On the other hand, I've known him buy a useless song or a gag to help a struggling writer. I liked Max.

'The season at Brighton was very hard work. With a change of programme weekly, and very little rehearsal, we played to the gag line. If a sketch began to drag a bit, Max would whisper to the artists ,"Close it up! Close it up! They'll never know." Then if the show underran he'd make up the time with his front-cloth act.'

The Brighton and Hove Gazette noted Jean Kent or Jean Carr as she was known then.

'Everybody liked Jean Carr, whose charm, youth and versatility are three graceful steps on the way to George Black stardom. Jean has a graceful presence and an appealing personality and she has taken everything in her dainty stride, especially in the Embankment scene where she played up to Max Miller with delightful style.'

Guest artists included Doris Hare and her sister Winnie Braemar, the dancer Jack Stanford, the comic, Al Burnett, Monsewer Eddie Gray and the coloured act Scott and Whaley.

The season closed on 16th November 1940 and for the first time in his career Max had a taste of pantomime. He was a guest artist in a pantomime given at the Comedy Theatre in London, sponsored by the *News Chronicle* in aid of the Rest Scheme for Civil Defence Workers.

London was going through the worst of the blitz and after a bomb hit the Holborn Empire, fortunately after the audience had left, George Black could see no alternative but to close all his London theatres, a policy confirmed by officialdom, in consideration of public safety.

By March 1941 Black had the go-ahead to reopen the Palladium, and the one artist who could fill that vast theatre was Max Miller. Wisely he revived *Apple Sauce* which had a record run of 462 performances, bringing Florence Desmond and Vera Lynn into the company.

The Times stated : 'This entertainment is none the worse for not quite making out its claim to be a revue. It is something many people like better—a good music hall show, thoroughly alive from end to end and all the glories of a multitudinous chorus added to its more homely attractions. Mr Max Miller and Miss Florence Desmond sustain the show's pretentions to revue status by appearing many times, but they are never altogether themselves until the time comes for them to top the bill in their familiar but unstaled turns.

'Only then does Mr Miller's joke—he has only one joke, though he makes it go a wonderfully long way—threaten to bring the house down, and his disarming laugh with all the reckless humour of the poor streets in it rings out on its true note. And only then do Miss Desmond's victims writhe. Her early mockery of an octogenarian charmer of the Parisian night stage carries so few guns that it is put out of action by the spectacular background. Her still earlier burlesque of Eastern romance seems an unwise condescension. Miss Vera Lynn's songs may be a trifle sugary to a sophisticated palate, but they are of the kind that simple sailors and soldiers home on leave like to hum.'

The Rev Edward Motley wrote with a memory of Max at this time :

'He kindly came to give a performance for the twelve hundred people who sheltered during the blitz, beneath the church of St Martin-in-the-Fields where I was a curate. I was deputed to look after him when he arrived to give his show. He must have noticed the look of perturbation on my face, for he said, "It's all right, padre, I'm not going to give my usual stuff tonight." '

Mr A Matthews saw *Apple Sauce*.

'During a performance of *Apple Sauce* at the Palladium there was a nasty air raid, but the company carried on regardless. Max asked if anybody would go on the stage and do a turn to keep up morale. I volunteered and after I finished one song, the house asked for an encore. I remember Max saying, "The Germans are all right over the Channel, but tonight they are in the wrong place. Go home Adolf !" What a comedian Max was—nobody could touch him !'

Max travelled up from Brighton every day. Miss Jessie L Davey wrote to say she was a registered escort for blinded troops at St Dunstan's.

'Despite Max Miller's busy hurly burly life during the war, he often found time to rush madly into the lounge of St Dunstan's saying, "Clear out girls. I've only got a few minutes." In no time we would hear the twang of his guitar and the men laughing uproariously at Max's risqué songs, and joining in his version of "Not for ladies' ears" war songs.'

The juggler, Billy Gray, did his act in *Apple Sauce* and also appeared in sketches.

'Meanness comes into most discussions involving Max Miller. I'd say he was of a saving disposition. I told Max that I'd like to give him a pony I called Rudolph. I took it down to Brighton by train and he met me at the station. Max didn't want to pay my fare or that of Rudolph. He did, eventually, and he had a good laugh about my worried expression !

'During the run of *Apple Sauce* at the Palladium, Max would bring up sandwiches from Brighton. Then he'd borrow a jug from the stage-door keeper, go over the road to an Italian restaurant, and get sixpence worth of tea.

'I decided to give up smoking and I gave Max two boxes of expensive cigars I'd kept aside for myself. "Thanks a lot, Bill," said Max. "I can't tell you how glad I shall be to be able to smoke a cigar again."

'I often worked the Empress, Brixton, with Max. Occasionally, he didn't want to go home to Brighton, so he'd bring up a camp bed and sleep in the dressing room. Next morning, he'd get up and go round the corner to Lyons' teashop and have his breakfast.

'Max liked to join in other acts on the same bill. I was just a juggler, and it made me very proud when an artist as great as Max said, "Can I work a gag in the course of your act, Bill?"'

Max did his duty as a fire watcher at the Palladium. He spent most of the time dictating answers to his fan letters, perched on the roof of the theatre. George Black's secretary would later type out the letters to await his signature. They were then posted for Max by the management. By way of repayment, the girl was given a cup of tea—occasionally.

In December 1941 Max was to be found in Trafalgar Square aiding the waste paper drive. 'When you buy tonight's supper on the way home, put the fish and chips in your hat,' advised Max. 'I can see men in this crowd wearing paper dickies. Put that dicky in the waste paper sack and wear a shirt—it's warmer.'

On the closure of *Apple Sauce* in December 1941, a new

revue went into the Palladium starring Bebe Daniels and Ben Lyon. Tommy Trinder, who was in the company, said:

'Here I am at the Palladium and Max Miller's at the Finsbury Park Empire. Time marches on.'

Miller was angry and his solicitor demanded the deletion of 'the objectionable gag.' When he was told to use a reprisal gag, Max replied, 'I wouldn't mention Trinder's name.' Instead another letter arrived from his solicitor asking for the exact words of the Trinder jibe—and he was told. He wrote to ask the date on which the joke was alleged to have been made—and he was told. He wrote to ask if it was the first or the second house—and he was told.

'I knew these letters were costing Max Miller six-and-eight a time,' said Trinder, 'and he wouldn't like that at all.'

In another Palladium show Trinder mentioned the name Max Miller. A stooge in the stalls got up, carrying a brief-case and shouted, 'I protest. I am Max Miller's solicitor.'

Max Miller clearly over-reacted to the publicity Tommy Trinder was giving him. He need not have bothered. Trinder had found a *niche* for himself in revue and pantomime. Max retained his position as our best front cloth comic.

His position in the profession was assured. Graham Greene paid tribute to him, adding, 'He would be revolting if he were not conscious all the time of what he is at.'

Max was always assured of a tremendous welcome at the Brighton Hippodrome. W Kennard Head saw him there when he was stationed at Lewes.

'Arthur Tracy, "The Street Singer", was on the bill. He was relying strongly on a microphone and he explained away his husky voice, "Sorry but I've got trouble with my throat." In other words a sanctimonious appeal for sympathy from the audience, who were only there any way to see Max Miller. I saw the show on the Wednesday and promptly booked myself in to see the second house on Saturday. On the Saturday show Max missed his place on the bill, but the show went on and Tracy did the same chat excusing his sore throat. Then Max's number went up and he made his entrance to the strains of "Mary From the Dairy." Max then did the funniest take-off of Tracy's sore-throated singing I have ever heard. Afterwards I spoke to the stage manager in the bar and he said Tracy was in the wings "shaking with rage".'

John S Vinden caught Max's act at the Chelsea Palace.

'There was a terrible fog that night, contributing to the small audience in the theatre. The "smog" penetrated the auditorium and when Max appeared a voice from the circle shouted, "I can hear you, Maxie, but I can't bloody well see you." Thereupon Max said, "Let's make a party of it." He invited the whole house to sit in the orchestra stalls and he then proceeded to perform at his best.'

Max wanted to keep up his London appearances and he played at the Empress, Brixton, and two 'off beat' dates, the Regal Cinema, Marble Arch, and the vast Stoll Theatre in Kingsway in May.

In October 1942 Jack Hylton and Tom Arnold jointly presented a stage version of a popular radio show, *The Old Town Hall* at the Winter Garden Theatre. Max, as guest artist, stole the thunder with two spots featuring his act.

With standing-room only notices out for Max's appearances at the Chiswick Empire, the Finsbury Park Empire and the Chelsea Palace, George Black decided Max was just the man to fill the Palladium again with the closure of a revue there. Max opened in August despite an increase in prices—thirteen shillings —the highest ever charged for an auditorium seat on a variety programme. Max lived up to his reputation as a crowd puller. He was making much capital out of the blueness of his material. Heading the first variety programme at the Palladium since 1939 he occasionally went over the top of propriety.

In 1939 Max had a series of humorous articles, including gags, ghosted for him in *The Leader*. This paper criticised him four years later.

'Now Max has never been a comedian you would expect to see at a Primrose League concert, but all the same after hearing and laughing at his gags at the Palladium, I wonder if he was being allowed to be too blue. Some of his stories are, in my humble opinion, just plain, unadulterated smut, others are merely vulgar, all have more than good helpings of double entendre ... There were moments in Max Miller's turn when I felt a little sorry for the people who had brought youngsters along to see the show. It is a certainty that Max would never be permitted to unleash his suggestive jests on the radio. He would have to tone most of them down and thereby spoil them from his point of view if he recorded them for the gramophone. Yet, paradoxically, he can put them over with impunity to the thousands of people who visit the London Palladium. I cannot support my suggestion that some of Miller's bawdy yarns should be barred by giving you examples. The editor wouldn't let me print them!'

The *Evening News* was less critical.

'Much as you may deplore Max Miller's determination to build his fun on the innuendo of sex relationships you have to agree he is irresistibly funny in himself, and a comedian with a definite pattern. Miller is the only artist of convincing stature on this bill, including Billy Cotton's band and Anne Shelton, a comment on the paucity of music-hall talent as we used to know it.'

The bill remained unchanged for eleven weeks. Despite the fact the bulk of Max's act had been familiar for years, he was still able to deceive an audience into thinking he was not as black as prudes painted him.

Max had a dispute with the BBC over unscripted gags he inserted into a live broadcast from the Holborn Empire in 1940. Four years later he began to tell a gag, which he later insisted he was going to modify, when the BBC producer, in a panic, faded him off the air. It was the same gag which got him in trouble when he cracked it at the Chiswick Empire.

'I was walking along this narrow mountain pass—so narrow that nobody else could pass you, when I saw a beautiful blonde walking towards me. A beautiful blonde, with not a stitch on— yes, not a stitch on, lady. Cor blimey, I didn't know whether to toss myself off or block her passage."

The dispute resulted in a BBC ban on Max Miller which lasted five years.

George Black made a grave error of judgement in booking Old Mother Riley and her daughter Kitty, known as Lucan and McShane, to top the Palladium bill. They were too provincial for the West End, and at the first house on Monday, troops, who were invited in free of charge, filed out of the theatre, giving a potent stamp of disapproval at the fare.

Max was always a riot at concerts for war workers and troops and he received many fan letters from servicemen. An airman, Sergeant Pilot Robert Rose of East Dulwich was killed in action. His will included two unusual bequests : £20 to the boys of his battalion 'to be spent on a binge' and 'my sports coat to Max Miller'.

George Black, in a quandary about how to fill the Palladium after Old Mother Riley's flop, re-engaged Max Miller, who topped the bill for twenty weeks of 1944—the longest run for a variety artist at this theatre. Max described the delights of Lulu.

> 'Lulu, I wouldn't fool you,
> I'm always saying nice things to you.
> I'll take you in the country
> Each Sunday for a trip,
> And as we climb the hills
> I'll walk behind in case you slip.
>
> Lulu. I wouldn't fool you,
> I'll take you to the seaside
> In anything I say or do,
> Not very far from town,
> And as we lay upon the sands
> We'll both get nice and brown,
> And if the sun should scorch your back
> I'll always turn you round—
> I wouldn't fool you, Lulu.'

Max had advice for 'Mary Ann'.

> 'Mary Ann, Mary Ann,
> Let us get together on the five year plan.
> We'll both go off to business
> Every morning, 'twill be fine,
> I'll bring my wages home
> And maybe you'll put your bit to mine.'

Despite his success, Max had to wait eight years for a return engagement at the London Palladium, where his season ended on 13th May 1944. The day before the *Evening News* carried this report :

'Huge salaries are being paid at present to a small group of entertainers—there are not very many of them—who can draw audiences into music halls. I have just been given some figures about these salaries by Mr Julius Darewski, the variety agent.

'The highest paid music-hall artist now is Max Miller. In one week at the Coventry Hippodrome recently Mr Miller earned £1,025. It is quite usual for him to receive £700 or £800 a week.'

After a week's rest Max appeared at the Empress, Brixton. At the Finsbury Park Empire in June, *The Stage* observed, 'Business proves there is only one Max Miller.' This trend was followed at other dates including Nottingham, the Metropolitan, the Lewisham Hippodrome and the Golders Green Hippodrome where Mr F M Barrett was present.

'It was during the doodle bug bombing. The air raid sirens sounded as Max was half way through his act. We all heard a buzz bomb approaching. Max carried on with his entertaining patter until the thing must have been overhead and that was a bit too traumatic, even for Max. He suddenly paused, and looking upwards, shouted, "Go over ! Go over !" It did, and the laugh Max's remark provoked was more from relief than anything else.'

George Black died in January 1945 and his responsibilities with the General Theatres Corporation and Moss Empires passed to Val Parnell. Soon the Palladium bills were headed by American artists.

Max Miller began a slow but sure decline in his professional status. He was a victim of circumstances; yet he made little effort to reverse the trend.

9   Films 1933–1942

THROUGHOUT ITS HISTORY the British film industry has mishandled some important talents that came its way. Max Miller and Sid Field were two of many outstanding artists who floundered because they were placed in bad pictures. The Americans knew how to assess an artist and then find the right script and the most suitable director to exploit his talent. In Britain if they hit on a good formula they flogged it for all it was worth. For example, the 'Carry On' series.

W C Fields, Charles Chaplin, Dorothy Parker, James Thurber and Mark Twain, people who successfully capitalised being funny, have stated that the basis of humour is tragedy, taken playfully; that is, you laugh hardest when you feel most sympathetic.

George Formby and Will Hay found the experience they gained in variety was helpful when they entered films. They each hit on a character which appealed to the public and could be placed in a string of similar stories based on nit-witted muddlings and humour through the midst of disorder.

George Formby's amiable Lancashire acquiescence made him the number one British screen comedian. In one film his sympathetic comic character was summed up in a song which had a direct bearing on the plot, concerning George as a man too inefficient even to be accepted as an ARP volunteer: 'I'm no wise guy, still I get along. I may not know my left from right, but I do know right from wrong.'

Will Hay was the headmaster of St Michael's—an imaginary

seat of misdirected learning. He was a seedy, disreputable character. The mortar board set at a rakish angle on the head, the
dusty tattered gown, the glasses sliding down an alcoholic nose,
the sniff, the sidelong glance and the sudden geniality of mis-
placed confidence, endeared him to audiences. Hay, like Formby,
found a rich vein of comic and peculiarly English characterisation. In other films Will Hay shed his cap and gown to become
a convict, a fireman, a policeman and a lawyer, but the character
was constant.

Max Miller was not so fortunate. He was unable to retain
the down-to-earth fun of his stage personality and use the possibilities that the wider canvas of the screen afforded a comedian.
Max became a smart-alec in films, always very much on top.
You can't feel sorry for smart-alecs. Only once was he able to
contradict that maxim—when he played the character created
by Edgar Wallace—Educated Evans, a perky tipster. This film,
which was immensely popular, exploited amusingly the effrontery
in which Max Miller specialised.

While Max maintained his popularity on the stage, his films
covered their cost, but were not popular with the bulk of cinema-
goers. They had two complaints. They could not hear him properly. He was always the cocksure braggart. After making fourteen films he was dropped by the industry. It was a disappointing
end to a career that began with an impressive boost from the
critics. His three minutes' appearance as a music publisher's
agent in *The Good Companions* suggested to most people that
Max had a great future ahead of him as a screen actor. The
year was 1933.

Max described his early film career with an unusual degree of
modesty.

'One night I was asked to go to a Gaumont-British studio
party and someone wanted me to make a funny speech. So I did
—bringing in the names of a lot of people present, and making
them laugh all the time.

'Well, two years later the Gaumont-British Company decided
to make *The Good Companions* with Edmund Gwenn starring
as Jess Oakroyd. They were looking for a man to take the small
part of a song salesman. They got on to Julius Darewski and he
agreed terms for me.

'I'd never been in a film before, and I'd made up my mind I wouldn't go before the cameras unless I got a good part. When I heard the song salesman only appeared for about three minutes I told Julius I wasn't interested.

' "You've got to," he said. "I've signed the contract!"

' "I'll break it," I told him.

' "But you can't do a thing like that!" he protested.

' "We'll see," I said.

'Next morning I went down to the studio and I cornered Victor Saville who was directing the picture.

' "Hullo Max," he said, laughing. "Have you come to break your contract?"

' "Yes," I told him, "and no kidding."

'He looked shocked. "But you've got to play the part. It's all signed and sealed for you to do it one day next week."

' "I'm in Birmingham all next week."

' "Then I'll come and fetch you early one morning."

'What could I do with a persistent man like that? So I agreed. Early one morning they called for me in a car, raced to London, and rushed me on to the set.

' "Well, what do I blinking well say and do?" I asked Saville while I was blinking well blinking in front of the bright lights.

' "Anything you like," he said. "You're supposed to be trying to sell a song to the character played by that actor seated at the piano—John Gielgud.

'Well, I'd often had chaps trying to sell me songs, so I knew what to say. I just stood there and rattled it off.

'Gielgud gaped and everybody else laughed. They'd never heard anything quite like it before.

' "Try it again," said the director and got the cameras going.

'So I did it again with more or less the same words and certainly with the same snap and conviction. They gave me a cheque for thirty pounds and drove me back to Birmingham.

'The reaction of the critics and the public to my little bit in that picture was one of the biggest surprises of my life. It got me a contract with Gaumont-British and it also proved that I didn't have to stick to the exact words of a script to be able to put over a performance.'

The film moguls could not decide on how to develop Max Miller's career as a screen performer. Instead of commissioning scripts tailor-made for a character of a Cheeky Chappie, they decided to give Max small parts and see how he developed.

Max's second part was in a film called *Friday the Thirteenth*. This concerned a number of people who were in a coach crash. The clock turned back to reveal incidents which had led to their being involuntary partners in a misfortune. There was a strong cast including Edmund Gwenn, Emlyn Williams, Gordon Harker, Robertson Hare, Sonnie Hale and Jessie Matthews.

Max played Joe, a light-fingered vendor in the Caledonian Market, trailed by a detective and two American assistants. *The Picturegoer* said of the film, 'It is a series of interdependent sketches none of which is really dramatically holding.'

Max's third appearance amounted to a disastrous miscalculation. The picture was called *Channel Crossing,* and starred Matheson Lang as a crooked financier. The entire action took place on a Channel steamer and Lang was going abroad with his secretary, played by Constance Cummings. Edmund Gwenn, Nigel Bruce and Dorothy Dickson also battled gamely with an inept script.

The Picturegoer stated :

'One mistake is the introduction of Max Miller with his popular patter as a commercial traveller. It was incongruous and unreal in the midst of realities and the way it is excused—stepping off the boat he is asked if he is really a commercial traveller and he replies that he is Max Miller trying out new gags—is a blatant confession of its weakness.'

Princess Charming, which was released in 1934, was described by Ernest Betts as 'one of those dreadful British films which brought discredit to the industry. No Hollywood company would have made such an abomination.' *The Picturegoer* stated :

'This Ruritanian hotch potch which stumbles about between romantic comedy and farce without achieving the merits of either, is not Miss Evelyn Laye's big break. The dialogue is weak, and, at times, excessively vulgar. Much of the humour is derived from Max Miller's act.'

Once again, at a loss for how to handle Miller, they just dropped in a filmic treatment of his stage performance. This did nothing to further his new career, but it helped the production. *The Kinematograph Weekly* observed : 'The resourceful inimitable humour of Max Miller keeps boredom at bay . . . he ignored the story and put over his own act.'

In *Things Are Looking Up* Max had a supporting part as Joey. Cicely Courtneidge had a dual role as an equestrian owner of a circus upset to hear that her twin sister, a straightlaced school teacher, had run off with a wrestler. She took her place and ended up as the headmistress.

Films offered an actor a salary many times greater than the theatre or radio, but the medium demanded many excellences. Because a film actor was enlarged several times on a screen, he had to look perfect for his part. Films tended to create their own stars, and acting had to be naturalistic; stage experience was not necessary.

Films paid large fees on a daily basis, and many established stage actors began to accept parts which were much smaller than those they undertook in the theatre. However, by 1935, Max Miller was determined to star in pictures. He secured a contract with Warner Brothers' First National company for eight pictures.

Unfortunately Max was not ready to carry a whole film. He had learned his craft in the hard school of variety, and he could not adapt easily to a new medium. For years he had given ten minutes to get his act across the footlights. There was no chance to build up a situation, and even when he played in revue, there was no time for adding subtle touches to make a character a flesh and blood human being. Max's whole attitude had been governed by the fact that if he didn't jump in straightaway and say something funny, and then keep on getting the laughs, it was apt to go badly for him.

Max was a star of variety and he didn't accept advice readily. He was not prepared to develop a new technique, which, before anything else, meant slowing down his performance and speaking his lines in a conversational tempo. He continued to gabble away, blind to the first essence of screen acting—credibility. He failed to establish his characters as clearly recognisable human beings. It was always Max Miller saying, 'Aren't I clever?' So it was that only the very uncritical were interested in following his fortunes for an hour-and-a-half.

Max's screen career was financially successful but artistically it was a disaster. He did not photograph well : he had a round face, a large nose and a small cranium. He was no good as a romantic lead. Without his byplay with an audience, he ceased to amuse people. His raucous voice and his speed of delivery often rendered him unintelligible.

On the stage, standing against a backcloth, Max was the centre of attention. In films, his impact was necessarily diluted, with the distractions of locations and other artists. More serious was the fact that Max, out of that flowered suit, in ordinary clothes, looked commonplace. He came across as a brash, unsympathetic personality, and there was little to remind audiences of his engaging stage image as a cheeky chappie.

Max Miller's first starring role was in a slapstick comedy called *Get Off My Foot*, released in 1935. It was directed by an American, William Beaudine, who made the Will Hay hit, *Boys Will Be Boys*. Max played a Smithfield market porter who wrongly thought he was responsible for his friend's death. He ran away and became a butler for an impoverished family. He fell in love with the maid. By carrying the whole film on his shoulders, Max was pushed beyond his resources as an actor. The *Evening Standard* said, 'It's fairly clean without being remarkably funny. The constant repetition of the remark which is the film's title is an irritation.'

In 1936 Max Miller achieved his greatest screen success when he starred as Educated Evans. The script was based upon Edgar Wallace's famous racehorse stories. The film told the tale of a fast-talking tipster, Educated Evans, who bluffed his way into the confidence of a couple of social climbers, who gave him the job of training their racehorse. The fun came from keeping up appearances while at the same time he forestalled crooks more unscrupulous than himself. The production had the snap and sparkle too often missing in British film comedies of the 1930s and owed much to the director, William Beaudine.

With *Educated Evans*, and its sequel, *Thank Evans*, Max found his only tailor-made part in films. The cockney tipster, with his incorrigible cheerfulness, could not be put down. Who else could play the part? Unfortunately, no other role which blended with a fluid story line was found for him. The critics were enthusiastic :

Daily Mail : 'Max Miller makes a grand film. He is on the screen practically all the time and gives a glorious performance'.
Daily Express : 'Just now and then he stops for breath, and you see there are others in the film, but it isn't often, and they don't matter.'
Daily Mirror : 'I defy anybody not to laugh at Max Miller's interpretation of a racing tipster.'
Sunday Times : 'Max Miller has waited for this break to show that he is without an equal.'

When Max made his brief appearance in *The Good Companions* it seemed that his screen possibilities were evident. With *Educated Evans* he got the part he needed to make him as popular in films as in variety. He reached star rank. Receipts in London and the Home Counties were excellent, but elsewhere the public did not give him universal acclaim. They waited for a follow-on picture, with rave notices. This never happened.

Max was quick to latch on to the perks that went with screen stardom. He began to be featured in personalised advertisement campaigns. He was one of the comedy stars whose adventures were chronicled in strip cartoons in the children's comic, *Film Fun*.

Max Miller's next film after *Educated Evans* was a let-down. It was called *Take it From Me* for a time but was released as *Transatlantic Trouble*, in 1937. It presented Max as a garrulous boxer's manager who could not get fights for his tough but dunderheaded client. He engineered a scene in an American nightclub so that the fighting man came into prominence by knocking down the reigning champion. That didn't get the fighter a job, but the champ's rich and silly woman friend took a fancy to him. That led to rogueries aboard ship on the way to England, with the breezily alert Miller character outmanoeuvred by a siren.

The film got much gratuitous publicity when it had to be withdrawn from the programme at the Empire, Leicester Square at the request of Lady Fairhaven, whose name was used in the picture about six times; it was necessary to get the actors to re-record a similar sounding name to synchronise with their lip movements. The character, the foolish society woman, was enamoured by the boxer, played by Buddy Baer, brother of Max Baer.

Irving Asher, chief of production at the Teddington studios of Warner Brother's First National Pictures, was not satisfied with William Beaudine's handling of Max and assigned two directors, Arthur Woods and Reginald Purdell, for the next production, *Don't Get Me Wrong*, released in the summer of 1937. Max appeared as a 'human dynamo' in a carnival show who found an insensible professor on his hands because of a little carelessness in the application of his electric handshake. The professor recovered and told Max he was the fugitive inventor of a petrol substitute.

Max saw a fortune in the professor's find and bluffed a petrol magnate with crooked designs into financing the invention. Max ended up with a wild aeroplane flight to advertise the new fuel, in the course of which he realised he was gyrating in space with a lunatic.

The amusing script by Frank Launder was too long but Max's brisk impudence and quick chatter gave it an enlivening quality.

Max discussed this period of his career.

'I never paid much attention to the script. It was agreed that I put the speeches into the sort of words I could get across. Trouble was, actors can't do that sort of thing. They learned their parts like a parrot and it used to throw 'em when I didn't give them the exact cue. It became a case of booking actors who were bright enough in the upper storey to work a scene my way.

'I began to make a packet of money by playing the halls and filming in the daytime. But it was a sweat. For the month or five weeks I was on a picture I used to do two houses a night, get home about midnight, and then be ready on the film set the next morning at 9 am. It wasn't too bad when I had a London date, but when I was appearing in the Midlands or the South, it was terrible.

'I was making a few thousands in a few weeks, but in the end I came to the conclusion it wasn't worth the strain. So I made a vow I'd never try to do both stage and film work at the same time.

'I learnt a few things filming I can tell you. *Now*, I can ride a horse. In fact I can sit a horse over a water jump. But when I had to do it for the films, the horse jibbed and I went clean over his head. Bang went a couple of my best ribs and I had to finish the film in plaster.'

For the sequel to *Educated Evans, Thank Evans*, Max had a new director, Roy William Neill. The film was first shown in July 1938. The public wanted to see the character of the cheerful braggart again whose swift inconsequentialities got people chuckling by their sheer effrontery.

Max was still the abysmally unlucky tipster who sold certs to an unsuspecting public and claimed close acquaintance with owners, jockeys and trainers. Although a swindler in his own way, he exposed a racket for fixing a big race. There was a ludicrous police-court scene and a cleverly staged horse race in which Educated Evans's bewildered tout rode the winner to victory in astonishing circumstances.

These two notices were representative of the majority:

Evening Standard: 'Miller's machine-gun style is unimpaired. But his ammunition might have been better. Many of the lines lack the old bite. *Thank Evans* is bright in patches, but it is not as funny as the original picture.'

News Chronicle: 'Invention flags now and then, but on the whole, in its broad, unsubtle way, *Thank Evans* supplies a good deal of uproarious fun.'

Warner's producer Jerome Jackson, the director Roy William Neill and Max had many lengthy meetings pondering the problems of box-office variations, searching for a new script, walking warily with 'Yes men', wrestling with critical advisers about the relative entertainment value of one piece of silliness and another, before deciding to make *Everything Happens to Me*.

It was described in *The Monthly Film Bulletin* as 'somewhat thin entertainment', though Max's screen image as a cheapjack was played down to justify the title. However, he still lacked the sympathetic appeal of his rival, George Formby.

Max played an indomitable salesman of vacuum cleaners who pitchforked himself into the job of candidate's agent during a by-election in a seaside town. Finding the candidate had been playing tricks with the funds of an orphanage, Max deserted to the other side, having frantically ridiculous misadventures until everything was resolved.

In *The Good Old Days*, shown in the summer of 1939, Max Miller was cast as a travelling theatre manager in the times when actors were called rogues and vagabonds. It petered out in the rowdiest sort of slapstick and though some of the trade papers called it 'reliable popular entertainment', the dailies were not so enthusiastic, finding the film, directed by Roy William Neill, as less than funny.

Unsophisticated audiences laughed at the spectacle of Max, the flamboyant manager and his harried company in the pillory and stocks, and at a pie-eating contest which the stout leading man had to be pummelled into winning because, unknown to his colleagues, he had already eaten a hearty gift meal just before it was due to begin. A good chase, with everybody getting sooty, was a fitting climax to this rowdy film.

Paul Holt, in the *Evening News*, stated :

You have in your hands, next week, the fate of Britain's best patter comedian, Max Miller, as a screen performer. His new film, *The Good Old Days*, is then on view in London. You like him? The problem has been that for some time the great bulk of provincial customers in the land have not. They have two complaints :

1. They cannot hear him properly.
2. He's always on top in his films. He says here's mud in your eye, but he never gets mud in *his* eye.

To cure that, his sponsors have made him speak slowly and have injected some synthetic sympathy into his roles. Judge for yourself. For myself I claim roundly that Max Miller is like a hobbled horse when he speaks slowly, and he is like Mr Disney's wolf in mermaid's clothing when he is sympathetic. Max is a brash guy, and if screen fans do not like him as a brash guy, then Max has no place on the screen.

The above didactic flow comes from seeing *The Good Old*

Days. They dress him up in an old top hat, moth-collar coat, silver-knobbed cane, pretend he is a busker of 1839 vintage and ask us to believe them. A fat chance. We've seen W C Fields like that.

Mr Miller, we know, wears red, white and blue plus-fours; he leans over the footlights, and likes to talk to any fattish lady in the first two rows. Particularly if it is hot. Then he will pluck at his plus-fours meaningly.

He will tell all who care to listen of his successes with the lady who gave her telephone number to his dad, and is likely, if pressed, to recount his dates in the desert.

But sympathy? Such things are left for Charlie Chaplin and comics like that. When they throw soot in his face, ripe pears in his eye, it's like putting Charlie Macarthy in the corner.

Surely there's some place left for impudence on the screen?

Paul Holt had not overstated the crisis in Max Miller's film career. If his next film was not a big hit, Warners had decided to call it a day and drop Max from their future plans. At a loss for a story or a character for him to impersonate, they took the easy way out by letting him play himself and once again put across his stage act on the screen.

The film, *Hoots Mon*, was totally lacking in original ideas. The director, Roy William Neill, had crucified his star with one inept film after another. Max was not prepared to change his style. He was quoted in the *Evening Standard* as saying:

'It was as Max Miller that I became known in variety and I believe the public prefer the same Max Miller on the screen. Any attempt to alter my style might prejudice both my film and stage work.'

Hoots Mon was a vehicle for Max's jokes and Florence Desmond's brilliant impersonations, both of which were excellently put over. The slender story, which had a little slapstick to help it along, concerned Max as a variety artist who objected to Florence Desmond, as another artist, doing an impersonation of his act. After various vicissitudes, the film ended with them doing a successful double act. It was seen by the press in November 1939.

It was three years before Max was offered a part in a picture, *Asking For Trouble*, which turned out to be his last one. It was directed by Oswald Mitchell for British National at Boreham Wood. The plot was built round Max, who appeared as his usual self, chatting away at Niagara Falls speed.

Max was a fishmonger and a part-time bookie who fell foul of the police for taking bets. While making a run for it, he became entangled with the daughter of a general, out to escape an unwelcome marriage to a captain. Her father, who had set up the marriage, had not seen the captain since he was a youth. Max masqueraded as the unwanted suitor, a noted sportsman. Eventually he won a steeplechase for the general, and the hand of his daughter.

Asking for Trouble was not a box-office success, and the British film industry lost interest in Max. He was forty-nine, past the age for playing a saucy bloke who chatted up the girls.

There was an option open to him : to abandon the idea of appearing in pictures written to fit his stereotyped image, in favour of character roles as they came along. This could have meant a loss of status, with co-starring or feature-player billing. Max was too conceited to lower his sights.

In any case, I doubt if Max was a good enough actor to be acceptable in the sort of cockney character which made Ronald Shiner a living in British films.

Max decided to quit the film industry while he was still a star.

As with his film career Max Miller never made much headway as a recording artist. His sales did not compare with those of Gracie Fields and George Formby. Essentially, Max's act was visual. Furthermore, the lyrics of his numbers were similar, the music lacked a catchy flavour. They could only be appreciated in performance as an essential part of his act.

However, Max made forty-nine singles, and in later years three LPs. He began his recording career in 1935 with a talking and singing disc, 'The Confessions of a Cheeky Chappie'. From 1936 until 1950 he recorded for HMV and most of the numbers were comic. His memorable records were made in theatres during performances—at the Holborn Empire, the Finsbury Park Empire and a modern classic, 'Max at the Met' (Metropolitan), made in 1957.

10 Marking Time 1945-1950

AFTER THE WAR there was little rejoicing; shortages and rationing had to continue and it was clear that several years of austerity must lie ahead. The USA was the land of plenty and the British public grasped everything they could feed us, including artists, good, bad and indifferent, known here for their screen appearances or records.

Gracie Fields was alone in maintaining her popularity, but she went into semi-retirement. Other British artists, popular before and during the war, were regarded as vestiges of a period audiences wanted to forget, and most of them drifted out of the limelight. There were exceptions.

The ageing Crazy Gang, who put across predictable and laboured antics, were fortunate in becoming entrenched at the Victoria Palace. George Formby, no longer a film star, retreated northwards, where he made a comfortable living. Robb Wilton kept a select following. There was nothing ephemeral about the target of his humour, which mocked hollow pretence at efficiency. When he busied himself in a fire station, it was not the fire service, but the whole of officialdom he satirised. Don Ross supplied nostalgia for the 'twenties and earlier when he toured *Thanks for the Memory*, featuring old-timers including Gertie Gitana and G H Elliott.

Ronald Frankau was one of dozens of artists who was dismissed as dated. A bald Etonian, he went to the limit in his use of suggestive material and he was popular with the smart set of the

1930s when he appeared in West End cabaret and revue. Playing to a wider audience as 'the blue boy of variety', he was less successful.

Jimmy James, who twenty years previously starred in a revue with Max Miller in support, was a superb droll who never received the recognition which was his due. He was incomparable as a drunk and as an ineffective man trying to organise bigger idiots than himself.

Broadcasting threw up its own brand of performer some of whom won quick recognition. A variety theatre booked to capacity for ten years would fall short in the numbers who heard one radio show. Tommy Handley was not a big stage star, but he established himself as a master of radio comedy. His premature death at fifty-five, in 1949, robbed the profession of a great individualist whose show 'Itma' remains a classic. An inmate of a postwar seaside hotel bitterly criticised the landlady. 'Why stay here?' asked Handley. 'I'm her husband,' the other shrieked— foil to the imperturbable.

Max Miller had many suburban and provincial bookings fixed when peace was declared. He was to attract capacity audiences drawn from those who knew him in his heyday. Young people were in the minority and many of those looked upon him as an interesting vestige from another age.

Things were not as healthy as Max supposed. Like many great performers Max was content to rest on his laurels. He avoided experiment, despite radical changes in the presentation and content of variety.

The development of sound amplification produced a new type of entertainer. Artists had no need to project their voices; they murmured into a microphone with a sexual intimacy. Talbot O'Farrell, a vocalist popular in the 1920s and 1930s, scorned its use and would point scornfully at the mike, saying to his audience, 'Look at it; God's gift to a crooner.' O'Farrell, like other artists of his generation, who played outwards and upwards in the tradition of variety, looked dated.

Having survived the multiple shocks of the bioscope, silent-feature films, dance halls, organised sport, talkies and radio, although much depleted, the theatre managed to maintain its fabric. With the reopening of BBC TV and the beginning of

ITV the structure began to collapse. Novelties, including stunt extravaganzas, drag and strip shows represented a temporary reprieve, and scores of theatres closed down. As Max Miller's appearances became less frequent, he told the press he was in semi-retirement to spite the tax man. In reality the opportunities were not there.

Kathleen Miller recalled a prestige engagement just after the war ended.

'Max received a summons to appear at Windsor Castle. He was asked to entertain at an enormous party their Majesties were giving for their staff, as a token of their appreciation for their loyalty during the war.

'After some difficulty Max was released for the Monday opening performance at the theatre he was working. He ran a Ford at the time, because of petrol shortages, and the journey took longer than he anticipated. There was a hold-up when he arrived. His invitation was issued in his real name of Sargent and the guard didn't recognise Max. Eventually Max got in and he asked an equerry what sort of show he should give, knowing that the Princesses Elizabeth and Margaret were to be present. "Do whatever you think is suitable, Mr Miller. The Princesses will not listen to anything they don't want to hear." Nevertheless, Max only used gags from the white book for that performance.'

Out of the blue Max was given a brief engagement in a variety season at the Prince of Wales Theatre in London's West End in August 1945. The press was enthusiastic, although the *Evening Standard* scolded Max for using material 'familiar for years'.

The *Jewish Chronicle* observed : 'To watch Max Miller as he begins a story, steals a sidelong glance at the auditorium, pauses, gives a wry smile, then starts again in an entirely different vein— all this is an education in true artistry.'

James Agate wrote in the *Sunday Times*: 'Max Miller promises his audience an essay in the Rabelaisian, though he puts it more simply. Like Lear threatening to say such things— what they are, yet he knows not; but they shall be the terrors of the earth. And then, wisely, this brilliant and subtle comedian does not say them.'

Then back to the road, taking in Brighton's Hippodrome, the

Finsbury Park Empire and the Brixton Empress, where he caused much amusement instructing the pit orchestra on how to interpret his number 'Josephine'.

When Max played a week at the Metropolitan, Edgware Road, in December 1946 he introduced a new number, 'While You Wait'. Roy Denton was in the bar with him when a man said he had a gag for sale. He wanted to know the going price. Max said, 'If it makes Roy laugh I'll give you a quid.' It did.

Max introduced the gag into his act and it got a big reaction. During the interval he sought out Roy Denton again. 'Have you seen that man who sold me the joke?' Roy said that he had left the building. 'Pity—that story had 'em falling about and now I can't remember the bloody thing.' Neither could Roy.

The relationship between Max and Julius Darewski was always a good one. At the beginning of the year Darewski would book Max with all the major dates on the Moss Empires and Stoll circuits and the smaller companies, although he could not break down the barrier and get him Palladium seasons.

Julius Darewski was also father-confessor for Max—he would brush aside Max's worries, including the one that Trinder was booked at the Palladium by Val Parnell to spite him and that Trinder's act owed much to him. 'He's miles apart from you, Max—different as chalk from cheese—nothing to worry about.'

Darewski was a shrewd man. He booked Max the week George VI died. 'With the BBC playing solemn music all day—you'll make a packet.' Max did. Once when Bertram Mills' circus was at Birmingham—it was to be expected that Max would not do such good business. In a rare moment of philanthropy the booker at Moss Empires, Cissie Williams, offered Max a guarantee. 'No, we don't want favours. Max will take a percentage,' said Darewski. He did and netted a record sum that week.

Julius Darewski had a fund of stories about Max and many of them reflected his admiration. 'Who else could turn his back on an audience for thirty seconds and still keep them laughing? I remember standing in the wings with Max and we watched a couple of superhuman contortionists grunting and groaning as they tied themselves in knots and tore their ligaments asunder to hold the attention of the audience. Max said, "Blimey—look at 'em. Too lazy to learn a comic song, I suppose." '

Barrie Darewski, nephew of Julius, was once in the audience at the Finsbury Park Empire and Max brought him into his act.

'I've got my agent in tonight, ladies and gentlemen. Name of Darewski. Here, Barrie, pop up to Harringay and see if Billy Graham is using any of my material, will you?'

The Darewskis often had complaints from the LCC and other bodies about alleged obscenities introduced by Max into his act. A transcript of the questionable jokes would be submitted, and on paper, without Max's leer and telling pauses, it was often impossible to read anything objectionable into the material.

Once when Max was in a despondent mood and said that when the BBC reopened their television service it really would be the kiss of death to variety, Darewski said, 'They'll still turn out in the rain to see you, Maxie.' They did.

Barry Anderson was assistant manager at the New Cross Empire. He remembered an incident in 1947.

'I was standing in the foyer one evening when I spotted a young soldier and his girl friend, who was in ATS uniform, looking at the front-of-the-house pictures of Max Miller.

' "Do you like Max?"

' "We've never seen him," said the boy.

' "Well, are you coming into the first house?"

' "We'd love to, but it's not possible."

' "Why?"

' "We're broke."

' "I tell you what," I said. "I'll pass you in if you meet me in the bar between houses and tell me what you thought of Max."

'I went up to the dress circle. Directly Max appeared the girl began to giggle and he had such an effect on her she couldn't stop laughing throughout his act.

'I went back stage to see Max and I told him about the couple and the girl's reaction. He said, "Let's see if they are in the bar." Sure enough they were there.

' "So you're the laughing lady of New Cross," said Max. "That's good for business." He peeled off a fiver from his wallet : "Go and have a good meal on me, kids."

'A little later I was in the foyer, and the same couple were queueing up, ready to use part of that fiver to see the second house.'

It was at the New Cross Empire that Max found a devoted fan in Flo Weller, a flower seller with a pitch in Bermondsey. She liked Max so much that until his very last London performance in 1959 she followed him to the other variety theatres, sometimes going twice in one week. She then began to go as far afield as Brighton and Reading. She met Max on several occasions. 'He was a very kind gentleman, but he didn't have much to say. He seemed to come to life on the stage. You couldn't beat him. He looked lovely too. I used to send him a box of biscuits every Christmas.'

In October 1947 Max was booked into the London Casino at the head of a good bill. Lionel Hale, unwittingly, wrote what many people were to quote sixteen years later as the most fitting epitaph for Max: 'The pure gold of the music hall.' The notice appeared in the *Daily Mail*; Max immediately adopted the description for his bill matter.

'There is no arguing with Max Miller's complete comic authority. How few are left in the music hall, when the straight stage and the BBC have sucked the life blood out of it. Max Miller is not very refined, but he is the pure gold of the music hall. He is the highest of low fun.'

Max returned to the Casino for a fortnight in August 1948. He was quoted in the press as taking a 35 to 40 per cent share of the box-office takings, which could have netted him a thousand pounds a week. It's doubtful if he made that figure, though the reaction was reasonable; he was the first British artist to top the bill there after fourteen months of foreign talent.

Leonard Mosley wrote in the *Daily Express*,

Max Miller walked on to the stage at the London Casino last night in a white hat and a suit of puce silk plus-fours, waggled a glass-topped stick at the audience, and shouted, 'There will be no dollars going out of this theatre tonight.'

We all applauded. We were happy to see a British star once more at the head of a West End variety bill. But in the next twenty minutes there were moments when I doubted his humour.

Where recent American visitors succeeded by the ease, friendliness, and clean harmlessness of their lines, Mr Miller gambles for success on carefully contrived songs and dances, a smart alec manner, and jokes that are 'blue'.

He appears to be proud that, by a twist of a word or the absence of a gesture, he can tell a story that your maiden aunt might not understand, but which you understand only too well.

The way Max Miller sees it, all the world is a smoke room. We laughed, and saw it that way too—while he was on the stage. But I came away hoping that there are British as well as American variety acts which still believe in good clean fun.

The Times headline read, 'Mr Max Miller's chilly efficiency.'

Mr Max Miller's presence in the new bill at the London Casino cannot suppress the reflection, long and hopefully put aside, that our music hall as a whole is in a pretty poor way. Mr Miller himself is a disappointment to those who recall the hopes awakened by his performances ten or twelve years ago. For he has arrived at the head of his profession without finding it necessary, even for his own satisfaction, to alter the formula of his act. The mild audacities, the boldly knowing smile, the cheery little snatches of song, the gaily coloured garments that made him seem a cockney bird of paradise: nothing has changed, except that the extraordinary personal relationship Mr Miller contrived to establish with his audience is replaced on his part by a faultless and chilly efficiency and on ours by a feeling of regret.

Max could not deny the truth of that notice. He used the same gags for years and he rarely featured a new song. However, one innovation crept into his act. Roy Denton recalled it started casually.

'Max borrowed some of his wife's clothing to walk on and off for a one-line gag. He moved like a real tart, and he had the perfect come-hither look on his face which paralysed the audience.'

Vernon Drake, of the well-known act Connor and Drake, was often mistaken for Max's brother, and they made capital out of their likeness. Vernon Drake recalled that Max made an appearance as a lady of doubtful years with his act at Folkestone. 'He was hysterically funny—he had the audience falling about with laughter.'

Billy Gray recalled Mark Molloy, who did an act in a dress suit, playing the piano.

'A beautifully groomed woman was seated at a second piano and they began to play a duet. Eventually the woman got up and walked down to the footlights. Everybody realised it was Max. He said, "I'm fed up with this lark." He took off his blouse. He wore nothing underneath, and he revealed that his skirt was held up by a pair of striped braces. There was a roar of laughter.'

The actor Sonny Willis knew Max at this time.

'At the Finsbury Park Empire an attractive woman arrived at the stage door to see Max. She asked him for a signed photograph. He autographed her programme instead. In the course of conversation she said, "You're much taller than you appear to be on the stage, Max." "Really?" replied Max. "But it's still the same length lying down as standing up."

'At the Kingston Empire the call boy was dressed up like a bell boy at the Savoy Hotel. He wasn't as polite or as efficient as Max would have liked and when it came to the end of the week he received a tip of threepence from Max, who said to me, "That boy will spread that story around for months—and publicity is good for me." '

As a young boy I found Max Miller kind. He once telephoned with the offer of a week's work.

'I've got a little stunt for you, son. Be at the theatre by 5 pm on Monday. Right?'

I arrived, and as I walked through the stage door I heard the sound of someone strumming a guitar from the direction of the stage. I found Max, seated on a stool, rehearsing to an empty auditorium.

'Hello, son,' he said, pinching my cheek gently with his forefingers. 'I've got a costume to fit you in my room. I'm going to dress you up as a pageboy, see?'

'Yes, sir.'

'Well, this is what you're going to do. See those two legs on the side there?'

'Yes, sir.' There were two legs, severed at the hip, and encased in black trousers. On the feet were black boots. They were obviously part of an outfitter's dummy.

'I shall be saying something like "I wonder who I shall do tonight, 'Mary From The Dairy' or 'Annie, the Farmer's Daughter' ". Or I may say "Josephine". I mean I don't know who I'm going to be fancying by that time, do I? Well, anyway that's when you come on and say to me, "Hitler's left leg, sir." Then get off, see?'

'Yes, sir.'

'Then there'll be a bit more patter, something like "I was walking down the street and this young lady comes up to me and says 'How do you do?' and I said 'Do what' and she replied 'Please yourself.' "That's when you come on with Hitler's right leg, see?'

'Taking the initiative, I said, "And I say, 'Hitler's right leg', do I?"'

'Yes, but no,' said Max. 'Can you roll your arse?'

'I think so.'

'Then you can roll your r's. Like this—"Hitler's r.r.r.r.ight leg!" I'm generous, I'm giving you a laugh line, son. Try it.'

'R.r.r.r.right leg.'

'Marvellous!' said Max.

On the night I did everything as rehearsed and after I made my second exit, Max produced two potatoes from his pocket, and to a roar of laughter, began to juggle with them. Then, with his masterful sense of timing, he snapped back, 'No, you're wrong lady, King Edwards!'

1948 and 1949 were critical years for Max Miller and he re-called his worries about his position in the profession.

'It seemed that there was no place for me in the West End. Let's face it, I never fitted well into scripted shows or pantomime. I always avoided long engagements like summer seasons—variety was my caper.

'I could still pack out a theatre, but the people that came in were mostly the over forties. I was too old to start changing my act, so I reckoned a good solution would be to try and attract younger people in to see me.

'Radio was the answer. I broadcast for Radio Luxembourg in

1948, then I got Julius Darewski to find out if the BBC still operated a ban on me. He thought rather than make a big issue of it, he'd try and book me in quiet like, and he pulled it off with an engagement on "Fanfare" from the North Region in August 1949. It was my first broadcast for five years.

'Then Henry Hall announced that he was going to revive his famous Guest Nights and he's such a good bloke, he agreed to book me about once every month, according to my stage commitments.

'There was never any talk about "Don't be a naughty boy again, will you?" They just checked out my script and I was on my best behaviour. I slipped one gag in and a woman split herself—I remember saying, "Don't laugh like that, girl, or I'll be off the air again." '

Everybody waited for him to say something awful. He didn't. Henry Hall explained Max's appeal.

'Max didn't like to be tied, but I managed to get him regularly on my Guest Nights. Because of the BBC ban he was quite new to many listeners. Despite the disadvantage in not being able to see Max, his superb confidence, and the way he had of using his magnetic voice, won him a new public. You could say he had the personality touch. He was so clever with the way he told a gag and left it to the listeners to decide on the meaning.

'It's for the producer to cut off somebody if he offends decency. There was never any trouble with Max. Mind you, we went through his material very carefully before the broadcasts and cut out questionable lines.

'Max wore his stage costumes for the broadcasts and that helped the studio audience reaction. It got him away to a good start. Max once said to me, "A comedian has got to sell a funny line to the public. It took me twenty years to become a good salesman."

'It was too late to worry Max with technicalities of broadcasting. To give him too many directions could have thrown him. As you know he had a habit of leaning forward and confiding to the people seated in the stalls. That could have caused problems. It was arranged, unbeknown to Max, that there should be double microphones—one nine inches away and one a foot

away. We picked him up on the second one, thereby allowing
him to project his act.

'One reads about the greatness of Dan Leno and Marie Lloyd
—but that was hearsay. For me, Max Miller was among the
very greatest. It was a privilege to work with him. He was the
master of his craft.'

1950 was to be the most traumatic year in Max's long career.
It opened well. Broadcasting increased his box-office appeal. A
zither song which began as a joke in his dressing room at the
Hackney Empire started up his recording career again.

Max said, 'Somebody came into my dressing room and spotted
my banjo and remarked, "Why not go on and say 'Come Hither
with My Zither?' " I did and it went down well and a bit later
we worked on the idea.

'Come hither with your zither
And play to me, a melody
In any key.

Come hither with your zither
And play a tune,
And I will swoon
Right into your arms.

It's the new sensation, though it's very old
My heart needs some warming
'Cause it's very cold.

Come hither with your zither,
And make all my dreams come true,
And I will swoon
Right into your arms.'

HMV offered to make a record of this number with 'I Never
See Maggie Alone' on the flip side—Max's first disc since 1942.
The *Evening News* of 25th March 1950 carried this report:

At the Chelsea Palace crowds were still going into the
second house ten minutes after the curtain had gone up.

Heading the bill was our old friend Max Miller. There wasn't one empty seat in the theatre. Yet I wonder if you'll find him in any of the Palladium programmes this year? I doubt it.

Now fifty-six, Max is something of a law unto himself. For instance, most top-line stars go on last act but one. Not Max. He closes the first half, insisting on catching the 10.25 train home to Brighton. He came on at 9.10 at Chelsea; was off by 9.35. I shall be surprised if his cheque tonight is less than six hundred pounds.

He asked for this sum at Finsbury Park a fortnight ago. He was refused. So, taking a percentage from the receipts—'If I don't draw 'em in, don't pay me; if I do let me benefit'—is his way of looking at it. He received seven hundred and sixty pounds for the week.

In October Max was booked to appear at the New Theatre, Cambridge. Kathleen Miller takes up the story.

'He was chatted up in the bar by several undergraduates. One of them challenged him to a round of golf the next morning. It was to be a needle match and Max accepted. The undergraduate turned up in a bizarre outfit with an enormous bag of clubs—so full he could hardly pull one out. Max arrived punctually, dressed quietly in flannels and a sports coat and carrying only one club —an iron. The undergraduate was staggered and complained, "I don't think you're taking our game very seriously, Mr Miller." "On the contrary," said Max, "I'm taking it very seriously. I usually go round with an umbrella." '

There were packed houses for the week. Max was foolish enough to participate in an acrobatic act on the bill called the Karloffs. Max was fifty-six and to bear the weight of three men was a great strain, and might have brought on the heart trouble which resulted in his death.

Max strummed on the piano in a double act with a blind pianist, Alfred Thripp, whom he kept in work for seven years, often fighting opposition from bookers like Cissie Williams, adverse to engaging anybody with a disability. Max was no pianist and in order to play a duet he had to stick cue papers on the keys of the piano to tell him which notes to strike. Some students found out about this, got into the theatre, and removed these papers. Duets were out for Max that evening.

Max's patter, including an account of a visit to a nudist camp, provoked roars of laughter. He began by saying, 'They have all the men one side of the hedge and all the women the other. 'Cause there's a lot of beating about the bush.'

Max was booked to make his third appearance in a Royal Variety Performance at the London Palladium on 13th November 1950. He was justifiably annoyed at being given only six minutes by Val Parnell, although Jack Benny was allowed twenty minutes, with an option of going over if he so desired. Max told his agent Julius Darewski that he would spring a surprise, but the confidence was taken as a joke.

Max's welcome far exceeded that given to Jack Benny. He immediately abandoned the routine he had rehearsed of selecting gags from his blue and white books, and did a modified version of the act he had put over with such success at Cambridge. The royal party and the house in general roared with laughter. Max was over-running by five minutes when the stage director, Charles Henry, could be heard shouting from the wings, 'Come off, Maxie!' Max was thrown for a moment and shouted back, 'The others have had their chance. Let me have mine. The Americans do. Here's a fine thing!'

As he came off, Max was confronted by Val Parnell, and he repeated the threat he made at the Holborn Empire many years previously. 'You will never work in this theatre again.' Apart from the money involved Max gave much the same reply : 'Mr Parnell, you are seventy thousand pounds too late.'

The incident developed into a major show business row and hit the headlines. David Lewin, writing in the *Daily Express*, stated :

Who stole Max Miller's joke books is Music Hall's mystery of the year ... Max said, 'I was going to do my normal Blue and White book act ... When I got on the stage, I felt in my jacket pockets. The books had gone ... I was flummoxed. I fell back on the act I have been doing on the halls for weeks. It went on a bit longer than the one we rehearsed for the show. But what could I do?

'I hear they are mad because I overran my time. But it is like having your elbow jogged when you are writing. Everyone picks on Maxie.'

In the *Daily Herald* Max was quoted as saying, 'Two of my gags might have been misrepresented, one referring to Millionaire's Row and another one. But they were normal innocent features in the substituted routine.'

Julius Darewski was interviewed for the *Daily Telegraph*. 'It appears that Mr Val Parnell, organiser of the show, was annoyed because Max put on an unrehearsed act. This had caused him to exceed his time . . . it was all a storm in a teacup and Mr Miller is extremely sorry for any inconvenience that may have been caused. The two books are still missing. They may have been taken by some practical joker.'

Val Parnell's office issued a statement. 'Mr Miller did not do his act as rehearsed, and he also went considerably over the time allotted to him. That was why he was told to come off.'

R B Marriott, the distinguished critic of *The Stage*, summed up the affair.

'He was rebuked back stage for over-running his time and using material—part of his act for years—which had been considered unsuitable for the hearing of the Queen. It was odd at least that he was called to order on the point of time, because at least one other on that programme (Jack Benny) appeared to be allowed to go on just as long as he wanted, and without half of the success of Max, who brought down the house.

'This in a way was a fitting farewell to big time variety. Max made a big hit; he showed his independence of spirit; he was determined that his act should have a fair hearing; his personality was at its most natural, his art at its most expressive, in wanting to dominate that great stage on such an occasion. His friends and admirers loved him for what he did on that royal evening.'

Ten years later I was sitting on Marine Parade, Brighton, with Max and I asked for the true explanation.

'All right. But it's only for publication after I'm dead. Of course it was my decision from the time of the rehearsals that I was going to get a better share of the limelight. Blimey, by 1950

I'd been on the stage thirty-one years, why should the Americans get all the star treatment?

'It was typical of Parnell, who had it in for me for years. But I wasn't going to go cap in hand to him or his lackey, Charlie Henry. It doesn't pay in show business to be humble.

'If George Black had come up to me and said, "Max, do six minutes for me at the Royal Variety Show," I'd have been a good boy. You bet your bottom dollar he'd have got a big contract lined up for me on a nice percentage.

'I wasn't taking the "six minutes only" bit from Parnell, who'd kept me out of the Palladium since 1944. And as for Charlie Henry shouting at me! Blimey—if he hadn't been a sick man, and past his work, I'd 'ave punched his teeth in.

'I had a rough time in the 1920s and that made me a bit of a loner when I made it in the 1930s. The profession demands everything from a man and gives little in return.

'To me a theatre is a place for doing an act in front of an audience—I'm by myself, I've decided what to do, and it's up to me to succeed.

'In my spare time, the theatre and show business people are out—I want to get away from it all—driving my car, playing some golf.

'Don't get me wrong, though, I can't wait to get in that suit of mine, to hear the band start up with "Mary From The Dairy", and to walk on that stage.'

11 The Last Years 1950–1963

THE ROW BETWEEN Max Miller and the organisers of the 1950
Royal Variety Show took time to simmer down. Luckily Max
was under contract for a few dates and his agent, Julius
Darewski, gave out false information saying Max had numerous
offers here and from abroad.

Billy Marsh, of the Bernard Delfont organisation, which
frequently presented Max, remembered his first appearance after
the row. It was for a week at the Nottingham Empire.

'Max was most concerned as to how he would be accepted by
the public. He wasn't at all sure he'd be well received and he
was worried. He had the idea that if one of the turns on the bill
would come into his act, it might be a help to him, and they
were quite happy to assist him. It wasn't necessary. He came on
to the stage to a tremendous ovation and he went over as big as
ever.

'Max learned that this particular act he chose was running
its own pantomime in a small theatre at Portsmouth and he said
he would appear during the run. "Put my name on the posters."
They were truly grateful because it meant sold-out performances.
Max kept his word and afterwards he said to them, "The favour's
returned."

'At the end of each week that I booked Max into a Bernard
Delfont show he would say, "We had a good week, eh? You'll
never lose money with Miller." However, once at the New Cross
Empire business was poor, and on the Friday I found Max hold-

ing court in the bar. He looked up at me and said, "I've had a worrying time, business hasn't been good." I replied, "Well, Max, it can't be helped, we've made a profit up to this week."

'Max said, "This is no good to me," and he insisted on going to the manager's office and telephoning his agent, Julius Darewski, to say he wanted to take a cut in salary, so that he'd be able to say, "You'll never lose money with Miller," and this he did.'

Max was heartened when the BBC invited him to appear in an important broadcast, 'Festival Variety', to mark their contribution to the Festival of Britain. An all-star cast included Gracie Fields, George Robey and Robb Wilton. Transmitted from a BBC studio, the audience consisted of employees of the Corporation and their friends.

The fact Max had been banned for five years by the BBC was obviously overlooked, but there was a roar of laughter when Max told the audience he had performed 'without the slightest sign of vulgarity.'

It was a big American star however, who caused annoyance among top executives by giving numerous and blatant plugs for himself and the London Palladium.

Clarice Mayne, equally well known in variety and pantomime, appeared with Max in the film *Educated Evans*. In the 1950s she recalled her impressions of him.

'In that film he looked the part of a bookie to perfection. However, it is as a variety star that I have some fond memories of Max. Although he is Sussex born, he has the cockney slang to perfection. I remember when he started the blue and white book routine. People would say to Max, "That gag's a bit naughty—got that one out of the blue book?" That gave him the idea of the two books.

'For all his sparkling eye and roguish smile I wouldn't say Max is a worldly man; he can be very serious; there's much more to him than one sees on the surface. I know he was deeply troubled about the incident at the Royal Variety Show of 1950. Almost every pro felt for Max and the injustice of Val Parnell in giving an artist of Max's stature a mere six minutes.

'Late that night, after the Palladium had shut its doors, I saw Max. He sat down and cried. It will surprise people to know that

Max is a sensitive man and his status as an artist is everything to him. After over twenty years of stardom, he probably thought his whole future was at stake; that he wouldn't work again. You see, to Max Miller, to hold an audience, to stand alone on a stage, and make two thousand people roar with laughter, is everything to him. To stop working would be a living death to him.'

In September 1951 the *Evening Standard* had a piece headed 'Where's Miller?'

When are we going to see Max Miller on the West End stage again? Miller is one of the two British variety stars—Gracie Fields is the other—who can top the bill at the Palladium and fill the house. Yet it is nearly a year since Max last appeared there at the 1950 Royal Variety Show. On that occasion Miller remained on the stage five minutes longer than his allotted time, despite a call from the wings to 'Come off!' There were subsequent explanations and apologies—but Miller has not been offered a Palladium starring date since then.

'Max has been so busy elsewhere that he wouldn't have had a free date anyway,' said his manager (Julius Darewski). 'He's getting booked up for next year too—including some Odeon cinemas.'

Well, I'm glad to know he's so busy. But isn't he missing the West End lights, as we are missing him? I think he and Mr Val Parnell should get together and show willing on both sides. A year is long enough—too long—to atone for five minutes' overtime and a few moments of lost temper.

Parnell gave way to pressure and offered Max a three-week contract at the Palladium in March 1952. With the headline 'A row is ended' the *Daily Express* recalled the Royal Variety Show row of 1950 and ended by quoting Max: 'You needn't be bad friends with anyone in this business.' And Mr Parnell: 'All is forgiven. This is kiss and make up.'

In a more detailed report in that paper, David Lewin stated:

'Everything round me seems strange.

My memory is not of the
    best;
I once got the sack,
But now I am back—
I'm playing once more in
    the West.'

Max Miller in a new flowered silk suit will sing those words on Monday night to announce that not only Mr Miller but variety is back in the West End for a new season.

I welcome his return. For Max Miller spells professionalism the real 'bang it right back at the customers' act of music hall. And professionalism has taken a back seat lately.

Says Miller : 'I had fifteen years learning the business before I got to the top. You need that experience if you're going to stay. Today, radio can give you a star name in four weeks. But radio stars, without music-hall experience, can feel very isolated when they try to top a bill on their own.'

'I know what he means. It is professionalism again. Even at the Palladium, where Miller is going, it has been lacking. Dorothy Lamour, Donald O'Connor and Larry Parks had big names—but little experience to mould a satisfactory act. They needed 'stooges' : Miller needs only an audience.

In those comic suits which most other comedians gave up with the red nose, Miller goes pattering on with the familiar routine of fast, sly jokes capped with a popular song.

The Stage of 21st February 1952 stated :

Hard work, a great affection for his job, and a faculty for always appearing fresh and enthusiastic have helped to make him what he is today ... He quite coolly knows something of his true value as all good artists must. He realises that popularity, if it is to last, must be merited.

'My comedy is the natural, homely, comfortable sort that brings everybody together. People recognise in my work, or so I hope, everyday feelings and happenings familiar in their own lives.

'These days I go on several times during a performance simply because I like it that way. After all you can get your applause only once. The intimate contact that can be established by this means seems to me to belong to the very spirit of variety.

'I like my audiences—and I feel all the better and work better when I find they like me. This may explain why I welcome interruptions. Then I can hit back with a quick gag. But I think it is important to know how far to go with this sort of gag, a technique that may take years to learn.'

Mr Miller stresses the necessity of catchy songs with a human touch to the variety comedian of today: 'They are as vital as ever they were, yet oddly neglected,' he said. 'In the past songs were always closely associated with variety, and many stars were for years identified with the songs they made popular. I regard my own song "Mary From The Dairy" as one of my most valuable assets and I'll go on singing it as long as I feel it is really wanted.'

Originality and the capacity to be yourself are essential to the artist who wishes to build up a steady, lasting popularity. "Stealing ideas and material and copying other artists never did any good," Miller said. 'I'd say to the young performer who is making his way: concentrate on trying to find out just what you can do; work out your own individual style. Then do all you can to develop yourself.'

A dame impersonation is Max Miller's latest addition to his repertoire. Recently he tried it out at a provincial hall and he then brought it to the Metropolitan, where it was immediately accepted as one of his most amusing comedy creations.

Max had a warm reception at the Palladium from the public and the critics. *The Stage* stated:

On Monday at least the cheers of the audience were reserved for Max Miller. He was given a really friendly welcome. He tells a few new stories and we have revelled in most of his gags before. But the brilliance of his feeling and approach as an artist makes all he does and says appear fresh and surprising. His asides, mock grumbles when applause comes too soon, and a dozen other Millerisms are a delight and all belong to the pattern of a robust comedy act that stands alone.

The *Daily Express* said :

> The Britons who took their acts to Broadway returned to the West End last night to open a new British variety season.
>
> Max Bygraves presents an Al Jolson medley; Michael Bentine jokes about New York; Anne Shelton sings American songs.
>
> It is left to Max Miller, who has not been to Broadway ('Too busy here, son') to appear, against a backcloth showing the old Holborn Empire, and shoot across a stream of vintage vaudeville gags.
>
> Max Miller's jokes are as flashy and smooth as his silk suit. He is irreverent, and revels in it. For those in the audience who insist on laughing at the more questionable meanings of his jokes, he has a short reply : 'You are the sort of people who get me a bad name.'

The Sunday press contrasted with reports over the Royal Variety Show row of 1950.

The *News of the World* then stated : 'The row which has followed Max Miller's appearance has grown out of all proportions ... To an Old Trouper it seems a pity to introduce acrimony into a great evening.' Referring to the 1952 season this paper said : 'Max Miller puts more into a roll of one eye than some can put into a whole act. "Max is back in the West" sang the Cheeky Chappie, who started off with a big laugh from those who remember his last exit. It was a droll performance, perfectly timed and expertly put over.'

The *Sunday Express* of 1950 was outspoken. 'What was so offensive was that in the presence of the Royal Family and before a distinguished audience, Miller put over the most suggestive routine I've heard in public. I don't want to sound sanctimonious. But this was cheap, grimy innuendo.' However in 1952 Logan Gourlay wrote in the same paper, 'Max Miller ... shows he has no rivals at cheekily winning applause.'

The *Sunday Graphic* of 9th March 1952, recalling the Royal Performance row of two years previously, said of George VI, 'He was privately delighted when one music-hall artiste at the

1950 Royal Variety Show strayed from a script specially vetted for Royal ears.'

Max's vital props seemed to have a habit of disappearing. Even though the story that he had lost his gag books on that vital night in 1950 was rubbish, he loved his diamond-studded cane which had been his prop for thirty years. It was stolen during rehearsals for his season at the Palladium in 1952. He was given a specially made new one by the management.

'I'm like a commercial traveller—ready for bed—any offers?' was one of Max's typical quips which endeared him to audiences at the Palladium. But let a lesser artist crack the same gag and see how it would die without a ripple on the waters.

In 1952 the BBC engaged Max to appear in a special Coronation Show on television, which was done as an outside broadcast on a boat going down the Thames. He was to be engaged to appear with Henry Hall on television and later in the 1950s when the commercial channel came into being, Max starred for Jack Hylton in his package shows fed into Associated Rediffusion's output.

Once Max rehearsed all day, then fell asleep in his dressing room. Somehow he wasn't called. An artist on the same show looked in minutes before Max was due in front of the cameras. 'You're on, Max!' came the shout.

Max woke up, rushed out of the room, fell down the stairs and sprained his ankle. He did his act in agony. Still the humour of the situation did not escape him. When the show was over he went to a restaurant with a friend.

'I'll have a steak and chips,' said his friend.

'I'll have a bread and poultice,' said Max.

'You'd Never Believe It' was the name of the series which starred Max. He did his act and appeared in sketches. One had him as a commercial traveller in a romp in an Eastern palace.

In 1952 Max introduced a permanent spot when he came on dressed as a voluptuous woman and he convulsed audiences in a duologue with Stan Hardy, who had been playing 'bits' with Max for a year.

Charles Henry commented: 'It was always said of Max he couldn't act anybody but the Cheeky Chappie. I agree with that, but with one exception. Dressed as a lady of doubtful age and reputation he was very funny. It was a pity he didn't develop this act earlier on in his career.'

Max was not feeling well during the autumn of 1952. He'd booked into some bad hotels, there had been some cold nights in November and varicose veins had caused him discomfiture. He went into hospital for an operation in December.

A friend and manager, F J Butterworth, was due for the same operation and Max gave him some advice.

'You should have this doctor I know who lives down in Brighton. Marvellous he is! What he does is to put a clip one end of the vein, then another clip a bit further up; then he gets out his scissors and cuts the bit of vein out.' Butterworth was paling rapidly. 'This doctor—he throws the bit of vein over his shoulder, straight into a bucket—never misses. Then he puts the clip up a bit and starts over again. Out come the scissors, bit of vein —over the shoulder, into that bucket . . .'

Max enjoyed stringing people along, and mild practical jokes also appealed to him. One of Max's oldest friends was the magician Reg Salmon, who would join Max and two other valued friends, Beryl and George Formby, for holidays on Max's boat, moored at Henley. Max's wife hated boats and the river and never went on these jaunts.

Reg Salmon had these memories of Max:

'I've never known Max to be down in the dumps. He bought a cabin cruiser, I'd meet him near Reading and we had many happy times with Max at the helm.

'One day I heard a mighty splash, followed by a muffled "Help" from Max. I rushed over and saw Max's linen hat floating right side up on the water! I immediately lay down on the deck to get it and look for signs of Max, when I heard Max behind me, roaring with laughter. For some reason I slipped and Max ended up rescuing me.

'On the stage I do a trick using a frame and three enormous playing cards, arranged so as to make a triangle. The audience sees the queen of diamonds, the queen of spades and the queen of clubs, and they are held up by assistants. After the suspense is worked up I say, "And here's the missing queen—the queen of hearts." As a rule a beautiful blonde makes an appearance. One night, right on cue, out comes Max, in his famous suit. Was my face red! Max—he's got a heart of gold—he's one of the best.'

The singer, Penny Nicholls, had this experience:

'I toured with Max in "The Max Miller Show". I featured a number "Hullo Mrs Jones", in which I telephoned "Mrs Jones" and told her all my troubles. During the act, Max would come on, put his arms around me and say, "Don't cry, dear."

'One night, unbeknown to me, Max made his entrance carrying a chimpanzee borrowed from another act on the bill. Suddenly I found the chimpanzee's arms around me!'

Max's florid suit and the whole idea of a patter comic looked sadly dated by 1953. Young comics, like Norman Wisdom, relied on singing and sketches. Yet Max was content.

'Thirty-five gags in ten minutes—that's still my style. Comics today haven't the material to keep up with that—even if they had the training. I bought my jokes when I was starting—I bought anything then to stop the other fellows getting it. I've got it all filed away in a cabinet.

'That's my Rolls-Royce outside. Does ten miles to the gallon, so I use the Lanchester for going around town. Oh, and then there's the De Soto for nipping up to the golf course or the river. Got the back arranged so it can take all my gear.

'I think all these fellows who want to croon like Johnnie Ray are ruining the business.

'I've got my boat on the River Thames. It's thirty four feet long and specially designed so I can handle it through the locks myself. I spend the summer in it. In the winter I do a week— then a week or so off. Got to look after my health, see? Income tax takes the money anyway. I still play on a percentage at a theatre. At Brighton I played to two thousand pounds. I get nine hundred out of it and tax takes seven hundred. I'm left with two hundred. That's enough.

'Then I've got my racing bike to keep me fit when I'm working. Put it in the back of the Rolls and go out on it every morning. Not up hills, though. I don't race up hills—bad for the heart, that.

'I'm not worried. People will come back to laughing at gags. There's no substitute for them in comedy.'

Who were the new comics who were winning favour? Frankie Howerd, given to expostulating, gurgling, and emitting howls of exasperated despair, was a flop when he appeared in the 1950 Royal Variety Show with Max. It took him fifteen years of ups and downs before he perfected his style and became a major talent of the 1960s. He shares Max's gift of establishing a rapport with his audience.

Benny Hill, a brilliant character comedian with an unrivalled sense of parody, has stated that Max Miller influenced him a great deal, especially in the comic possibilities of roguish charm.

'Big headed' Max Bygraves idolised Max Miller and adopted the name 'Max' for the stage.

Arthur English, a cockney stand-up comic, lacked Miller's charm and expertise, but achieved recognition with the gimmick of an extravagant 'spiv' get up as 'The Prince of the Wise Boys'. English stood in awe of Max.

'I was booked to star in a series of radio shows and I always took the last spot. One week Max Miller was the guest star. I knew I could never follow Max on a bill. I asked the producer to switch the running order to allow Max to go on last. I'd made the right decision. He went on and slayed the audience.'

Arthur English is now a successful character actor.

Despite these and other new and talented artists, there were dwindling box-office returns at variety theatres as more people stayed at home and watched television, and even three or four broadcasting and recording personalities on one bill failed to attract.

In 1953 Max played what was to be his last season at the Palladium and John Barber made these comments:

He entered from under the stage ("That's the kind of gags you're going to get—straight from the sewer"). And he joined a muscle-man act, the Three Karloffs, as the strong man who lifts the others.

'Surprises like this keep variety fresh. Too many artists last night worked old material. Only one thing is worse: imitations of American stars. Tessie O'Shea chose to guy Eddie Cantor and Al Jolson.'

A E Wilson, writing in the *Evening Standard*, thought Max 'was hysterically funny as an acrobat . . . he introduces bizarre elegance, a budget of new stories and a number of new ditties. With his knowing glance, his disarming air of innocence, he never allows you to forget he is the Number One "Cheeky Chappie".'

Albert Baker, who has already been quoted on his memories of Max as a young man (see page 38), was chief limes man at the Grand Theatre, Brighton, for nine years.

'The Grand was very much a number two date, and to my mind, it showed Max was going downhill when he played there and not at the Hippodrome.

'Part of the secret of his success was his attention to detail. In the early days when his wife paid threepence a yard for curtaining to make his flowered suits, he was not satisfied until they really looked good on him.

'He was always on the look out for new material—he'd buy a gag at the stage door and when I said to him, "Was that a good 'un?" he'd say, "It would have to be for me to pay for it. Dirty—blimey, I'm going to be delightfully filthy tonight."

'Max was a difficult task master—it was hard to satisfy him. He had a knack of turning his back on the audience and looking at the back cloth, to see if the lime was picking him up properly.

'Max didn't throw his money about. I went to repair a heater for him—and what he gave me, well, it paid my fare there and back, I suppose. He talked a lot about his wealth and the cost of his possessions. He dressed the part of a star and he would get a bit upset if people thought he was slipping.

'I remember he started driving a small car around Brighton and a woman questioned him about his Rolls-Royce.

' "Oh, I had to sell it, lady."

' "What—things not so good with you, Maxie?"

' "No, the ash trays were full." '

In 1953 Max was sent a song called 'My Old Mum' which was to be second only to 'Mary From The Dairy' in popularity. A comedy number on the joys of cycling—'Let's Have a Ride on Your Bicycle' was another winner and Max recorded them both on a single for Philips. This was to be followed by other discs which were poor; many of the numbers sounded like the worst in a bunch of publisher's rejects.

The entertainer Clarkson Rose recalled booking Max for the Eastbourne Pier.

'The directors were angry with me. "He's so vulgar and suggestive," said the managing director. "Don't worry," I replied.

"Max will do as I ask him." "Nobody will come and see him," was the retort. In point of fact he packed the place and broke all records.

'I explained to Max that I couldn't possibly afford his fee, but that he'd enhance my prestige if he would come. I know he wouldn't have minded me telling you he received what amounted to an expenses fee of thirty pounds at a time when his fee for such an appearance would never be less than a hundred guineas.'

Max Miller's name has often been linked with John Osborne's character of Archie Rice in his play *The Entertainer*, produced in 1956. Mr Osborne has said : *

'Some people have suggested to me that I modelled Archie Rice on Max. This is not so. Archie was a man. Max was a God, a saloon bar Priapus. Archie never got away with anything properly. Life cost him dearly always. When *he* came on, the audience was immediately suspicious or indifferent. Archie's cheek was less than ordinary. Max didn't have to be lovable like Chaplin or pathetic like a clown. His humanity was in his cheek. Max got fined five pounds and the rest of the world laughed with him. Archie would have got six months and no option.'

Max said, 'My wife went to see Sir Laurence Olivier after she saw him appear in *The Entertainer*. He said he was a great admirer of mine. Never met him myself. I understand he studied me closely before he played the part of this dud comic—to be insulted by Sir Laurence, that's a compliment in my book. I could have straightened him out on a few things if he'd asked me.'

R B Marriott of *The Stage* said :

'It is said that John Osborne's *The Entertainer* was at least partly based upon Max Miller. No doubt Mr Osborne studied Max's act very thoroughly, but Archie was, despite years of work, a failure, both as a man and as an artist. And this Max Miller certainly was not.'

1956 was a bad year for Max. He broke his neck when the engine of his boat misfired. As a result he was ill for many weeks and he had to refuse offers that came his way.

The 1950s saw a marked decline in Max's theatre bookings.

* *Observer* magazine, 19th September 1965.

He made an annual visit to most of the London Suburban halls and he was a particular favourite at the Metropolitan, Edgware Road. There, the hum which passed through the auditorium, when the number of his turn went up, was a well-remembered thrill which, among British artists, perhaps only Gracie Fields had the same power to evoke.

He used gags which were in his repertoire in the 1930s, and there was very little in the songs he introduced. However, the tang and bite of the whole performance was in the collective mind of the audience. He only had to remark, 'Last night I said to this girl . . .' and the house was in uproar.

The spirit of his performance was captured in his finest recordings 'Max at the Met', recorded on 30th November 1957.

For the 1958 Christmas season on BBC TV Max was ill advised in accepting the part of Idle Jack in a pantomime, *Dick Whittington*, with the title role being played by his colleague from *Apple Sauce*, Jean Kent.

Max was not happy at rehearsals and as Billy Gray, an assistant on the programme, recalled : 'Some of the supporting artists squabbled over funny lines and who should say them. It took Max to put these idiots in their place by saying, "Remember *I'm* the bloody star." '

Max, tied to an inept script, censored for the juveniles, 'looked as out of place as a publican at a Methodist garden party,' stated the *Daily Express*. He was.

In April 1959 Miller appeared in a season at the Palace Theatre in Shaftesbury Avenue—which was to be his last West End engagement. He found a new clean gag which he announced to the press before the opening.

'A fellow rings a Scotsman and asks to borrow a fiver. "I can't hear you," says the Scotsman. "Lend me a fiver . . ." "I can't hear you." The operator butts in. "I can hear him, sir." "Well," says the Scotsman, "you lend it to him." '

Max received a favourable press. Cecil Wilson in the *Daily Mail* wrote :

Max Miller, beaming at himself in a plus-four suit of violet-flowered lemon silk and a white semi-sombrero, is, as ever, music hall to the core. As he freely admits to one of the many women who misinterpret his double meanings, 'There'll never be another, will there, girls?'

At sixty-four he rattles off new gags and songs with all his old lip-smacking, eye-rolling cheek. His jokes are still more laughable than printable, his songs unashamedly corny, his dancing a model of conserved energy, his guitar playing an obvious joy to his own ears. His general tongue-in-cheek self approval remains irresistibly infectious.

I met Max a few weeks later and he was troubled by the decline in his status.

'Good thing I've put plenty of cash aside, isn't it? Got it all hidden in safe deposits, son, not to mention annuities for myself and the wife.

'I was really sorry when they finished variety at the Empress, Brixton, and made it a cinema. The Metropolitan is on the rocks and so are most of the halls in the provinces. Look at all of my old dates that are now TV studios—the Hackney Empire, the Wood Green Empire, the Shepherd's Bush Empire, the Granville, Walham Green, the Chelsea Palace . . . terrible, isn't it?

'As far as I'm concerned, I reckon the game's finished. Radio eats up material and they pay peanuts anyway. Television—that's the thing of the future, but it's not for me. I can't do my act too often on the box—it would kill my chances for the few theatres left. Anyway, one week in a theatre pays more than one television job, so it's not sensible, is it?

'Sketches and this so-called situation comedy on TV is out as far as I'm concerned. I don't come across doing that. What's more, I can't keep to a script or remember lines.

'Thinking up songs and gags keeps me amused. If I retire what would the other comics do for jokes, mate? But I want to get out while I'm still good—none of this playing on sympathy—"poor old bloke" bit for me I can tell you.'

Kathleen Miller described Max's engagement at the Finsbury Park Empire which began on 14th September 1959.

'Max decided to stay with his old friend, Reg Salmon, who lived a few miles north of Palmers Green. After the first house on the Tuesday Max had a severe pain in his chest, which he thought was due to indigestion, but it got so bad he could not move and he couldn't go on for the second house.

'How he drove his car to Palmers Green I do not know. Directly Reg saw Max he realised he was very ill and he called his doctor who immediately fetched an ambulance and he was taken to the Royal Northern Hospital just in time to save his life.

'I did not know anything of this until two-thirty the next day when the hospital rang, telling me that Max had a coronary thrombosis. They allowed him to say to me, "I'm all right, don't worry." I told him I would come up, but he got very agitated and said he would not hear of me travelling up to London alone. I could not argue with him. I did go up the next day, however, and Max was a little better. He returned home about a fortnight later.'

After a long rest Max was advised by his doctor to try a week's work. He had been pining for a chance to walk on the boards of a stage again, and where better than the Brighton Hippodrome? It was June 1960.

The Evening Argus stated: 'The cheekiest of all chappies, Max Miller, was given a great ovation when he made his comeback at the Brighton Hippodrome last night and he responded by giving twenty minutes overtime at the first house ... I am happy to report he is in better form than ever, combining the best of his old act with some devastating new patter he dreamed up in his hospital bed ... Many young artists could learn from this fine old trouper.'

'There's no one like me—there'll never be another,' said Max, and every night Brighton audiences, the most critical judges of variety in the country, greeted him like a long-lost friend. They never wavered in their support for the town's most famous comedian.

Max bought an Austin Princess car with automatic gear change and began to adjust himself to a new and quieter life. He met old friends in the bars and on 'the over-sixties seat' on Marine Parade near his home.

Although the notices for Max were kind, the bite and attack of his performance at the Hippodrome had lessened as an admirer, Edgar M Kingston, recalled.

'It was a poor imitation of the glorious act he did at the

Holborn Empire in the 1930s . . . the brash confidence of the man had evaporated. In the ground-floor left bar he said to the barmaid, "Give him a drink," pointing to me. "He always comes here when I'm on." Max was in women's clothes—that was part of his act which would have been unthinkable in the pre-war days.

'One evening I drove up Marine Parade and I found a traffic bollard had been demolished in the wide area of the road. It was about 6 pm. I stopped and Max Miller was on the pavement by his car. I summed up the situation, which must have been brought about by negligence. I said "res ipsa loquitor" (the thing speaks for itself—a legal maxim). Max grunted "Eh?" I explained the meaning. He appeared very depressed and hardly answered.'

Max made his last stage appearance at Folkestone in December 1960.

In June 1961 an executive of the Pye Record Company found Max on his boat near Shillingford and it was arranged that he would record an LP at the Black Lion Hotel, Patcham, near Brighton in front of an invited audience. Called 'That's Nice Maxie' it was subsequently banned by the BBC.

Max made another LP, 'The Cheeky Chappie', at the Star Sound Studio in London in September 1962. On both records it was clear his precision and zest had departed.

Max's sister, Elsie, recalled the last year of Max's life.

'He loved his work and to be forcibly retired, faced with long days and nothing to do, made him very unhappy. He would call in, and invariably he would sit and strum away on my upright piano. Occasionally he'd hit on an idea for a song. Then he'd say, "What's the use?"

'Once on his way here, his car hit a bike parked in the gutter. He stopped and the child was in tears. Max bought him a new bicycle.

'I'm not an observant person and I didn't know Max wore a wig. Once I touched his head and he was most annoyed. He wore the wig in hospital. In fact, although he was very ill, he kept up appearances until the end.

'Max had a full set of teeth. Just before he died he made an appointment with a dentist and asked him to pull out one of

his molars. The dentist examined Max's teeth and said :
' "But why should I extract a perfectly good tooth, Mr Miller?"
' "But I want to know what it feels like to have a tooth out."
' "That's a request I'll have to refuse," said the dentist.
'Max was a good man. He bought this house so I can end my days in comfort.'
In May 1962 Max received a letter from John Betjeman asking him to sing 'Sally in Our Alley' in the Egyptian Hall of the Mansion House during the City of London Festival.
John Betjeman's letter continued :
'You, in those shot silk plus-fours, are just the man for this job if you would be willing to undertake it. Will you? Anyhow, I am glad to have the opportunity of telling you that you are to me a great genius, as you must know you are, and have given me so much pleasure. I'd like to see you in this entertainment singing to the Queen, the Lord Mayor, and all those civic nobs.'
Max rejected the offer. He had already planned a fishing holiday.
In July 1962 Bill Worsley invited Max to do a broadcast from the Playhouse Theatre. Max decided to drive up from Brighton and in the course of trying to park his car he was drawn into a violent dispute with another motorist. Max calmed down, but no sooner was he in his dressing room than he collapsed with a mild heart attack. A doctor was summoned and he was advised to go into hospital. Max was adamant. 'I'm going to do the broadcast—that's final.'
Ron Lowes, who was the sound engineer on the programme, remembered seeing Max seated at the side awaiting his turn.
'It was very unusual for an artist to wear a special costume for a radio show. Max was dressed up in his stage gear—in the floral suit and the upturned trilby.
'He looked very weak, and it appeared that he didn't know where he was or what he was about to do. However, once he walked on the stage he seemed to come to life. Fortunately it was a recording and he did break down a couple of times. We did retakes, and the end product was perfectly satisfactory.'
The last time I met Max was in the autumn of 1962. It was obvious he was losing his grip on life. He had lost weight and as

he seated himself on his 'over-sixties bench' on Marine Parade, Brighton, he wrapped the loose folds of his overcoat around himself, and jammed his stetson firmly on his head.

There was a long silence and I realised that he did not want to talk. Below, the sea was rough and the billows clashed and collided with one another as they strove to find their level. Cascades of white foam sparkled and hissed as it followed the changing patterns of the surface. When a receding wave left behind a remnant of foam, it nervously washed pebbles on the beach.

Max began to speak, as if to himself. 'A couple of months ago you couldn't see that beach for people. Makes you think sitting here. Just along there I sang "Black Sheep of the Family" in Jack Sheppard's concert party. Knew I'd go places—didn't eat for a couple of days to afford that suit I wore.

'Look at them waves—full of hate they are. If I went down there, I'd be swept out to sea. What a way to go, eh? Nothing better, I'd say. I can see the headlines : Max Miller dies on the crest of a wave." '

Kathleen Miller takes up the story.

'Max went to London to discuss making a record with Lonnie Donegan and Pye Records. It was agreed that Donegan would come to Brighton to rehearse with Max on 4th November 1962. It was a bitterly cold day, with icy winds blowing.

'Just before Mr Donegan was due to arrive a neighbour called in to tell me she had spotted Max on the roof of our house. I rushed upstairs and called out, "What are you doing?" He replied, "Cleaning out the gutters."

'I begged him to come down. Max replied, very politely, to leave him alone and to wait for Lonnie Donegan downstairs. I was very glad when he arrived with his group. Max had to get off the roof and come downstairs. He enjoyed the discussion and he smoked a cigar which the doctor advised him against doing.

'After the record was made, Max only made one further public appearance—at the Dome, Brighton, for the 1962 Christmas Carol Service.

Percy Sargent recalled the last months of his brother's life.

'After the heart attack Max seemed to become a different person. He rarely spoke and he was very sad. Formerly he was always witty—but that ceased and he even lost the sparkle in his blue eyes.

'Max was a strange chap. He'd arrange to meet me in a bar and then he'd give me a pound. Before he actually handed it over, he'd squeeze it into a tight ball. It always took time to straighten it out and as I was struggling away he'd chip in by asking for a double Scotch. He'd get his pound back that way. My God, he was mean!

'I was living in a caravan and Max came to see me. He was driving a small car—he called it his invalid carriage. Poor old Max—he looked so ill. He was a peculiar grey colour. He complained about pains in his chest. He said, "I'll see you are all right, Percy. I'll buy you a house."

'I never got that house. Percy was never that lucky.

'Max said, "I'm going to give you two hundred quid in cash, Percy. "I'll get Kathleen to bring it round to you." She did, in an envelope. I counted it and there was only a hundred and ninety-seven. I said, "There's three quid missing, Kathy." She fished in her handbag and found the other three pounds loose.'

In the last week of April 1963 Max's illness took its final turn. Kathleen Miller remembered that Max was very disturbed about the thought of going into hospital.

'He begged me not to let him go into hospital. I nursed him myself, but he got far worse with every day that passed.'

Max's last words were 'Mum, oh, Mum!' and with that The Cheeky Chappie smiled, closed his eyes and was happy in his own blue heaven. Three minutes later, midnight chimed over Brighton and the very last peacock-coloured shred of variety was dead.

Kathleen Miller said, 'He was loved. Once I went to see Sir Laurence Olivier in *The Entertainer*, and he heard that I was out front. I was given a note to say he'd like to meet me after the show.

'When I went into his dressing room he just sat and stared at me for a long time and then said, "Mrs Miller, I'm a great admirer of your husband." '

On the day of the funeral Burlington Street was so crowded the police closed it for an hour. There were fifty-six floral tributes, but only a few from members of the entertainment profession, including Lonnie Donegan, Tommy Cooper, Jack Warner, Elsie and Doris Waters and the sons of George Black, George Jnr and Alfred. The people looking on, and the two hundred in the congregation at St Anne's Church, a stone's throw from the Millers' home, were mostly old age pensioners.

I remember Max Miller's last words to me a year before his death.

'People have got the wrong idea about me, John. They say I'm conceited. I'm not; in fact I'm quite shy really.

'Who's Max Miller when he's not on the stage? A nobody, mate. But the Cheeky Chappie, he's a great bloke.'

Epilogue

THOMAS HENRY SARGENT left an estate of £27,877 net. Everyone expected a six-figure sum given both Max Miller's earning capacity and saving disposition.

However, Max had invested in annuities for himself and his wife, and he confessed to me he had stashed away a considerable sum in safe deposits. He loved the feel of money and almost certainly a great deal lay unaccounted for by such means.

Out of the £27,877 estate Max left his house in Burlington Street to his widow, a villa in Hove to his sister, Elsie, plus £1,000, and £1,000 to his brother Percy plus personal effects.

Biggest surprise of all, was £7,000 to Miss Ann Graham. The will opened with this bequest : 'Miss Ann Graham, c/o Lloyd's Bank, 1 Church Road, Hove, £7,000 and all monies derived from the publication (excluding mechanical rights and recordings) of my songs in recognition of and in gratitude for a very long and happy partnership of song writing.'

This bequest came as a shock to Kathleen Miller. She immediately set about finding out what she could, but Miss Graham was the most discreet of women and to this day has remained incommunicado.

Max had few close friends or confidants. A man nearer to him than anybody else was Vic Saunders, who for over twenty years was his chauffeur. It was Vic who had to see that Max caught that last train back to Brighton every night and as the years passed, Max relied on him more and more for other journeys. To Kathleen, Vic Saunders was the obvious person to tell her about Ann Graham. She wrote and telephoned continuously, but Vic withheld information.

When Kathleen was questioned by the press, however, she affected to know all about Miss Graham. In 1963 she told the *News of the World*, 'She is a single lady of about fifty-five. She acted as his travelling secretary when I decided it was too much for me to dash about the country seeing theatres and so on. I'm glad he left her something. She thought she had been a great help to him.'

In fact Max had known Ann for over twenty years and she was his constant companion. She was tall, auburn-haired and well-educated. People described her as looking like a schoolmistress; Max had a penchant for women who wore glasses. She was pleasant and efficient, always keeping in the background. Everybody in the profession knew about her, but word never reached Mrs Miller.

By the end of the 1930s Kathleen had lost her grip on Max. He no longer invariably caught that last train. Vic Saunders mentioned that he would inform his wife that he must stay up in town over night. In reality he only wished to be in the company of Ann Graham.

In October 1950 Max played a week at the New Theatre, Cambridge (see page 150). As usual Vic Saunders had met Max at Victoria and then driven him and Ann to Cambridge—it was all part of a routine. On arrival at the theatre, Miss Graham, the perfect secretary, busied herself with Max's affairs. Max came off after his spot and said to Vic Saunders, 'These students love my stuff—it goes across very big, mate.' The atmosphere in the dressing room was a very happy one until the stage-door keeper shouted up the stairs, 'Mr Miller! Mr Miller!' 'Go and see what he wants, Vic,' said Max. The next thing Max heard was Vic Saunders talking in an unusually loud voice, 'Hello, Mrs Miller. Fancy seeing you here!' Ann Graham missed a confrontation by seconds and was back in London that night.

Alex Goad was a devoted fan of Miller's. He was good company and Max would invite him on his boat for weekends. 'I remember all three of us stayed at a hotel in Henley. Max was always on top form in the company of Ann Graham. Max liked to have his photograph taken—I remember a photographer came down when Beryl and George Formby were his guests. Ann Graham never allowed anybody to take a picture of her.'

After Max's death Ann Graham went into hibernation. An estimate of her affection and admiration of Max was shown when she sent a set of photographs of him during a performance to Roy Hudd. She enclosed a brief note, but no address.

Why has Ann Graham kept the secret of her love so long? Perhaps the public has no right to know.

As Others Saw Him

CHESNEY ALLEN:
'He demolished all barriers between himself and his audience; ordinary folk uderstood him immediately.'

ANONYMOUS TRIBUTE:
'Goodbye Max; your story's told.
You've taken your last calls,
And joined the famous stars of old,
Who made the music halls.
But folks who loved your breezy style
With jokes that made them happy,
Will oft remember with a smile
Their dear old Cheeky Chappie.'

ARTHUR ASKEY:
'He was the finest front-cloth comic I ever saw. As he said himself, "There'll never be another." He was magic.'

CHARLIE CHESTER:
'The greatest stand-up comic who ever lived.'

TOMMY COOPER:
'I thought the man was great. I'd never miss an opportunity of seeing him. You could see those blue eyes of his from the back

of the gallery. As an artist there was no one to touch him—marvellous.'

GRACIE FIELDS :
'Max always seemed to be a very happy fellow, but I never thought he was as happy as he tried to make out—he was a worrier. He was always trying out his gags on whoever he talked to; so often in fact that he became a bore to strangers listening to him. We theatre folk understood—he was trying to work out each gag to perfection. He never stopped working. He was a joy to see and listen to at the Palladium or the Holborn Empire where we were often on the same programme. There was no other comic like Max. He really had no need to wear those crazy and colourful suits, he was funny enough without the exaggerated get-up. In summary I'd say he was a proper love. No one has ever taken his place in the theatre. He was different. He was unique. We old 'uns miss him very much.'

BILLY GRAY :
'I worked on bills with Max for thirty years. From the moment I first met him at the Canterbury Music Hall in 1929, I thought this man has magic. He would walk on the stage, and without saying a word, or even moving, he would provoke laughter. Max would look up at the gallery and the reaction grew stronger. It seemed as if the whole world was his; as a performer he was perfection. You gave me so much happiness, Max, thanks a million.'

ROY HUDD :
'Max Miller was my childhood hero. I used to see him at the Croydon Empire and the Metropolitan, Edgware Road, and he summed up the sort of bloke I wanted to be—a flashy dresser, with that floral suit of his, even those brothel-creeper shoes—perfection ! He was a man who could pull all the birds; he had a few bob in his pocket and he always had a snappy answer. Max was a mixture of every flirtatious milkman, every fast-talking bookie and bar wit. He was the sort of fellow you'd like to have as your mate, because, next day, you could say, "By the way, have you heard this one that Maxie has just told me ?"

'When I went on the stage I began to analyse the man's appeal. He was marvellous with an audience. He used brevity in phrasing a gag. He sailed near the wind, and got away with it every time. I remember at the Croydon Empire he said, "I went into a chemist yesterday," and he got a huge laugh. The reason was Max Miller would only go into a chemist for one article. His songs were very much part of his act. They showed him off as "Jack the Lad". Then Max would slip in one about his love for kids, or his old mum, just to show he was a good bloke under the bravado. The word Chappie is dated nowadays. But for Max Miller, The Cheeky Chappie was the perfect bill matter.'

JIMMY JEWEL :
'Sid Field was the greatest sketch comic I ever saw; Max Miller was the king of stand-up men. Max had a technique nobody else had—of making a joke sound blue before he told it, and then it wasn't blue anyway.'

TURNER LAYTON :
'Max Miller was a giant among performers. I have yet to see an English artist have a vast audience rocking with mirth in the way that Max did—and often all he used was a sidelong glance, a slight gesture and a few well-chosen words. I saw Max countless times and I never ceased to be amazed by him.'

ALFRED MARKS :
(On the death of Max Miller in 1963) 'Music hall died twelve years ago, but it was only buried today.'

R B MARRIOTT :
'The music hall in which Max gloried and to which he brought the lustre of his genius, died before Max. Even if his health had been better in the last years of his life, and he had been eager to work, it is difficult to know just where he would have flourished, so much was he part of the traditional British music hall. As an artist and a man he won and deserved enduring admiration.'

ERIC MORECAMBE :
'Max Miller was the comic all comedians went to see. He established an immediate rapport with his audience, and in his act he gave a study in brilliant simplicity.'

LORD OLIVIER :
'Max Miller was a master comedian, striding boldly in a field of innuendo. It was not the innuendo in itself, particularly, that made him a master. It was the timing of it, and the placement of it, the encroachment of it.

'He was an extremely subtle study in boldness. Starting his routine in the mildest of ways, then dropping in some utterance that made us not quite believe what we had heard, and gradually and relentlessly increasing the pressure to an hysterical conclusion.

'Max Miller had me on occasion literally in the aisles. He was a great one, indeed, to members of the profession.'

JOHN OSBORNE :
'Max Miller was a popular hero more than a comic because he was a genius. All genius is a cheek. You get away with your nodding little version and the world holds its breath and applauds. Max took your breath away all together and we applauded.

'I loved him because he embodied the kind of theatre I admired most. His method was danger. "Mary From the Dairy" was an overture to the danger that he might go too far. And occasionally he did. God bless him. Hardly a week passes when I don't miss his pointing star among us.'

SANDY POWELL :
'Robb Wilton was the finest storyteller in the business and Max Miller was the finest gag merchant. People say Max was blue, he wasn't. I've known him walk on the stage and if he only looked at the audience in a certain way, he made it seem filthy. He'd say, "I said goodbye to this girl", and make it sound sexy. I worked with Max at the London Palladium in 1929 when we shared a dressing room at the top of the building. He went on and slayed the audience. Very soon he was back there as top of the bill. Max Miller was a great comedian.'

TED RAY:
'Max Miller was unique. He was a loner and not well liked in
the profession. He had a reputation for being mean. On stage
no other artist could follow him.'

CLARKSON ROSE:
'Max was not a man who mixed very freely in the profession.
Success and affluence often breeds envy and unjustified criticism
from one's fellows. Max often suffered from such injustice as
this and yet I happen to know his private benefactions and help
to those in need, were wide and generous.

'I was always completely convinced he didn't understand some
of the outrageous things he was going to say and sing. Max was
a mixture of cockney cheekiness and complete naïveté, and in my
opinion, it was this mixture which made his act—audacious as
it was—completely inoffensive to a healthy and broad-minded
aduience.

'There was none of the leer of the old-time comics—no red
nose and battered hat. The blatant silk and satins of his attire,
the immaculate stockings and shoes, perfectly groomed head,
and smart hat, tilted to one side, plus a winning and disarming
smile, was the cleverly concealed paraphernalia that made the
Cheeky Chappie supreme in his generation.'

TOMMY TRINDER:
'By the death of Max Miller music hall lost one of its great
personalities. He was a really terrific performer.'

BILL WORSLEY:
'When Max Miller died I felt a sense of personal loss. I suppose
I worked more than anybody else with Max at the BBC. If there
was any comfort to be gleaned from his death at the age of only
sixty-eight, it was that he would have been so unhappy as his
frequency of engagement would, inevitably, have tailed off as
the years passed by.'

HARRY WORTH:
'Max Miller was, undoubtedly, the best patter comic of them all.
His sense of timing was brilliant. I was on the bill with him at

the Finsbury Park Empire in 1959 when he had his heart attack. The day before he gave me a very old book on comedy which was kind of him. He made a deep impression on me; as an artist I have never seen his equal.'

Daily Telegraph :
'Miller remained faithful to his methods that had served him well, and as the opportunities for genuine music hall decreased, in later years, his stage appearances were relatively few. But by connoisseurs of his genre he will be long and gratefully remembered.'

The Times :
'Although he often appeared in films, on radio or television, his impact in these media was blunted . . . he belonged essentially to London and Brighton, and to the tradition of the individual concert party entertainer, whose virtuosity he developed to a fine art.'

Michael Grade :
'The true measure of greatness in music hall terms is said to be how well you go at the end of your performance. With Max there was never any question that he would have to "beg off". His unique and unmatched achievement was how well he always went before he walked on—the buzz, the giggling, the unmistakable feeling the audience emitted, suggesting that they were in for the time of their lives when the first chords of "Mary From the Dairy" struck up from the pit orchestra. "There will never be another," he used to say—there never has been.'

Appendix

Discography of Max Miller

In compiling this list I am grateful for the assistance of Michael Pointon, Jim Hayes of Disc Research, England, and Peter Lowe.

1. 78 RPM issues in order of release

Confessions of a Cheeky Chappie, pts 1 and 2 : Rex 8604 (Oct 1935)

Confessions of a Cheeky Chappie, pts 1 and 2 : Broadcast Twelve (another issue) 3266 *Plus* song *My Superstition*

Max the Auctioneer, pts 1 and 2 : Rex 8665 (Dec 1935)

The Woman Improver and *Mary From The Dairy* : HMV BD 385 (Dec 1936)

Ophelia and *Down In the Valley* : HMV BD 396 (Jan 1937)

Backscratcher and *Impshe* : HMV BD 408 (Mar 1937)

Why Should the Dustman Get It All and *You Can't Blame Me for That* : HMV BD 417 (Apr 1937)

How the So and So Can I Be Happy and *The Girl Next Door* : HMV BD 419 (May 1937)

The Love Bug Will Bite You and *Julietta* : HMV BD 427 (June 1937)

You Can't Go Away Like That and *Weeping Willow* : HMV BD 432 (Jul 1937)

The Windmill and *La De Da* : HMV BD 439 (Sep 1937)

Put It Down and *The Old Oak Tree* : HMV BD 450 (Oct 1937)

I Never Thought That She'd Do That To Me and *Let's All Have a Charabanc Ride* : HMV BD 458 (Nov 1937)

Voice Of the Stars—Extract from film *Don't Get Me Wrong* : VS4 (1937)

Just Another Sally and *The Christmas Dinner* : HMV BD 475 (Dec 1937)

Annie the Farmer's Daughter and *Ain't Love Grand* : HMV BD 482 (Jan 1938)

She Said She Wouldn't and *I'm the Only Bit of Comfort That She's Got* : HMV BD 505 (Mar 1938)

Winnie the Whistler and *Doh Rae Me* : HMV BD 533 (Apr 1938)

Every Sunday Afternoon and *Um Ta Ra Ra* : HMV BD 541 (May 1938)

I Bought a Horse and *Does She Still Remember* : HMV BD 563 (Jul 1938)

The Girls Who Works Where I Work and *Happy School Days* : HMV BD 583 (Sep 1938)

She Was She Was She Was and *Just in Fun* : HMV BD 597 (Nov 1938)

Max Miller in the Theatre : *At the Holborn Empire*, pts 1–6 : HMV BD 615, 616, 617. Recorded 24th Oct, 1938 (Dec 1938)

Max Miller in the Theatre Again : *Second House at the Holborn Empire*, pts 1–6 : HMV BD 646, 647, 648 (Mar 1939)

Everything Happens to Me and *At the Bathing Pool* : HMV BD 697 (Jun 1939)

No, No, No and *Maria Fell for Me* : HMV BD 710 (Jul 1939)

Max Miller in the Theatre : *At the Finsbury Park Empire*, pts 1–6 : HMV BD 770, 771, 772 (Dec 1939)

Max Miller with the Forces (Somewhere in England), pts 1–6 : HMV BD 883, 884, 885 (Dec 1940)

Max Miller Entertains the War Workers, pts 1–4 : HMV BD 980, 981 (Dec 1941)

That's the Way To Fall In Love and *When You're Feeling Lonely* and *She'll Never Be the Same Again* : HMV BD 987 (Jan 1942)

Max Miller in the Theatre (Finsbury Park Empire), pts 1–4 :
HMV BD 1022, 1023 (Nov 1942)
Come Hither With Your Zither and *I Never See Maggie Alone* :
HMV B 9878 (Mar 1950)
My Old Mum and *Let's Have A Ride On Your Bicycle* : Philips
PB 199 (Dec 1953)
Mary From the Dairy and *Voulez Vous Promenade?* : Philips
PB 236 (Mar 1954)
Two Little People and *Friends and Neighbours* : Philips PB
296 (June 1954)
Pleasant Dreams and *Oh Yes! She Knows Her Onions* : Philips
PB 274 (Oct 1954) (with The Beverley Sisters)
Someone Else I'd Like To Be and *Don't Forget Your First Sweet-
heart* : Philips PB 362 (Nov 1954)
London Belongs To Me and *Something Money Can't Buy*:
Philips PB 427 (Apr 1955)
The Budgie Song and *Ain't It Ni-ice?* : Philips PB 518 (1955)
The Girls I Like and *The Mother Brown Story* : Nixa N 15050
(May 1956)
Be Sincere and *With a Little Bit of Luck* : Nixa N 15141 (June
1958) (Also issued as 45 RPM 7N 15141 and on NEP 24076
reissue—only with *With a Little Bit of Luck*)

2. 45 RPM issues

Influence and *There's Always Someone Worse Off Than You*:
Pye 7N 15349 (June 1961)
The Market Song and *Tit Bits* : Pye 7N 15493 (Jan 1963) (with
Lonnie Donegan)

3. EPs issued

Mary From the Dairy and *Every Sunday Afternoon, Ain't Love
Grand* and *She Said She Wouldn't*—from 78 masters : HMV
7EG 8558
The Best of Max at the Met : Two Pye EPs, NEP 24154 and
24162

4. LPs issued

Max at the Met : Nixa NPT 19026 (Recorded 30th Nov, 1957,
featuring *Mary From the Dairy, Passing the Time Away, Be
Sincere, The Girls I Like, The Fan Dancer* and *Mary Ann*)
10 in. LP. Issued as 12 in. LP Pye Golden Guinea GGL 0195,
with extra tracks : *With a Little Bit of Luck, The Mother
Brown Story, Influence*. This Golden Guinea issue, reissued
on Marble Arch Mal 740, without *There's Always Someone
Worse Off Than You*. Issued as *Golden Hour of Max Miller* :
Pye GH 584; with all tracks listed above plus *There's Always
Someone Worse Off Than You*

That's Nice, Maxie : Pye NPL 18064 (1961) Reissued—Marble
Arch MAL 597 : featuring *Josephine, Twin Sisters, On the
Banks of the Nile, Hiking*

The Cheeky Chappie : Pye NPL 18079 (1962). Featuring *Lulu,
She Said She Wouldn't, Doing all the Nice Things* : Reissued
—Marble Arch MAL 1257; Reissued Hallmark HMA 240
with new title, *You Can't Help Liking Him*

The Cheeky Chappie : Philips 6382 114 (Reissue of old Philips
tracks) *Let's Have a Ride On Your Bicycle, Don't Forget
Your First Sweetheart, You Broke Your Promise, Someone
Else I'd Like To Be, Something Money Can't Buy, Little
Swiss Miss, Friends and Neighbours, Oh Yes! She Knows Her
Onions, London Belongs to Me, Voulez Vous Promenade?,
My Old Mum, Mary From the Dairy*

Max Miller in the Theatre : One Up 2075 (Reissue of *Max
Miller in the Theatre* : *At the Holborn Empire* : BD 615, 616,
617, 646, 647, 648)

5. Extracts of Max Miller on anthology albums

Hail Variety : Oricle MG 20033 (Extract from *Max at the Met*)
Music Hall to Variety (Second house) : World Records SH 150
World of Music Hall : Decca PA 81 (Rex reissue of *Confessions
of Cheeky Chappie*)
50 Years of Radio Comedy : BBC REC 138 (Broadcast extract)

Index